The Chess Game

by
Kevin Callahan

Dedicated to Donna and our children Mary and Jackson, and walking the streets of life with the three of them. Also dedicated to Msgr. Bob McDermott, Msgr. Michael Doyle and Msgr. Michael Mannion, who walk the talk they preach. The three Catholic priests walked and worked on the streets of Camden, dedicating their lives to helping the "least of our brothers" while anchoring the challenged city with hope.

Printed in the United States of America
Published December 2017

© Copyright 2017 by Kevin Callahan
All rights reserved worldwide.

ISBN: 0-9990372-6-9
ISBN-13: 978-0-9990372-6-3

All rights reserved. No part of this book shall be reproduced or transmitted in any form or by any means, electronic, mechanical, magnetic, and photographic, including photocopying, recording or by any information storage and retrieval systems, without prior written permission of the publisher. Although every precaution has been taken in the preparation of this book, the publisher and author assume no responsibility for errors or omissions. Neither is any liability assumed for damages resulting from the use of the information contained herein.

Cover Design: Joseph A. Martino
Interior Layout Design: Joseph A. Martino

For more information on this title please visit:
www.PUBLISHwithJAM.com and
www.CallahanServices.us

Acknowledgements

With deep appreciation to Denny Brown, Jim Catrambone, Jim Cummings, **Lesly D'Ambola**, Joseph Dowling, Harry C.J. Himes and Nancy Jerome who wrote reviews for *The Chess Game*.

I appreciate the guidance and expertise of publisher Joseph Martino, but mostly admire his courage and faith in the trilogy. I highly recommend him as a publisher and friend!

Thanks again to Barry Joseph, the great Baz, for reading this draft along with drafts of *The Black Rose* and *The Fish Finder*.

Appreciation and admiration to the people of Camden who have inspired me to write *The Chess Game* - Msgr. Robert McDermott, Msgr. Michael Doyle, Msgr. Michael Mannion, Sister Rosemarie Kolmer, Sister Helen Cole and Sister Karen Dietrich - as I've seen them dedicate their lives to helping the "least of their brothers."

Special appreciation over the years to the many others I've seen in positive action, including all the passionate and compassionate workers at the Camden County Prosecutor's Office, who help keep the city safe, to the many writers at the Camden Courier-Post, who help keep the people of the city informed, to all the dedicated teachers at

Camden Catholic High School, who help educate the youth of the city and to the basketball coaches at the Camden Partnership Schools, who help teach the city kids how to play and pray.

Thanks to my father, Jack Callahan, my brothers Rich, John and Paul, and sister Liz, who have all helped build homes for The Heart of Camden, for their support. An extra special thanks to my wonderful children, Mary and Jackson, who as young kids helped deliver Christmas baskets at Sacred Heart, and my brave little wife, Donna.

And with the deepest gratitude and admiration to my mother, Barbara Hayes Callahan, who when I first started *The Black Rose* trilogy over 20 years ago, read the first draft of *The Fish Finder* and responded with a note to tell me everything that was right with the story and the writing before appropriately concluding, "Kevin, this was a very nice try."

So, with the help of so many, this is my final try in the trilogy...

Book Reviews

The Chess Game takes you on an odyssey you won't soon forget. Callahan's grasp of the history, humor, and humanity that exist in the oft embattled city of Camden, New Jersey is nothing short of brilliant. Once you start, the pages seem to turn themselves.
   - *Denny Brown, Creator of the TV series CHASE STREET*

Kevin Callahan shines an illuminating light on what from the outside appears to be a dark place. There is a saying on a wall at Camden NJ's Romero Center that reads, "So you say you love the poor… name them!" This is the centerpiece of Msgr. Bob McDermott's work in Camden. *The Chess Game* not only puts us on the journey to know the plight of the people of Camden with greater intimacy, it challenges us to ask, "What am I doing that assists the poor and vulnerable? Can I call just one by name?"
   - *Jim Catrambone, Executive Director, The Joseph Fund of Camden*

Wow! Biblical symmetry not withstanding Kevin Callahan brings it home in *The Chess Game*. A tale of Camden, Oh Camden told through the eyes of the unborn child...of poets from today and yesterday; the trinities of corrupted mayors and priestly heroes. *The Chess Game* will physically

and literally walk you through this iconic American city that reflects a hopeful heart of a nation. It is a story of intrigue that captured me to the very end.
   - *Jim Cummings, Founder UrbanTrekkers and Urban BoatWorks, Youth Development Ministries with UrbanPromise Ministries in Camden, NJ*

In *The Chess Game*, Kevin Callahan brings you on a profound spiritual and historical journey through Camden, NJ – one of the poorest cities in America, and quintessential ministry field. *The Chess Game* keenly manifests the core tenet of Ignation Spirituality – finding God in all things. God is profoundly present in Camden, New Jersey!!
   - *Lesly D'Ambola, D.O., Former Medical Director of Saint Luke's Catholic Medical Services, Camden, NJ and Former Jesuit Volunteer*

Kevin Callahan's novel, *The Chess Game*, rocks with American and Irish soul.

An impactful story that fully absorbs the reader into main characters Cresty and Choker's journey through the streets of Camden, New Jersey which unfolds over the course of one summer day.

This day of exploration and searching for the King ("you mean The Wizard," as Cresty continually repeats) is Callahan's vehicle for magnifying his own American soulfulness and passion for social issues and consciousness.

And you will love the soundtrack! Cresty and Choker listen to and discuss the meanings of U2 songs over the course of their Beautiful Day walking the streets of Camden. Callahan artfully changes bits of the lyrics as he communicates to the reader on both conscious and subconscious levels.

Enjoy this thoughtful, seamlessly told story from the soul.

- *Joseph Dowling, M.S., LPC, Specialist in Peak Performance Psychology, and Author of ZONEfulness: The Ultimate Guide for Student-Athletes*

The Chess Game is the last book in a Trilogy by Kevin Callahan. All three books are a story unto themselves but sprinkled with anecdotes about the three main characters - a father, his daughter and her boyfriend. These three protagonists are in search continually for their souls; their meaning for existence.

The objective lens used by Callahan in his Trilogy gives the reader – no matter his viewpoint- a discerning and deep mystical-philosophical dive into three of the major culture issues of our day- Race, (*The Black Rose)*, Abortion (*The Fish Finder*), and Social Justice (*The Chess Game).*

The Chess Game takes place in the battered, and high crime rate city of Camden, New Jersey.

The young mother to be is mistaken about the time of her doctor's appointment which is at 8 PM and not 8 AM. She and the father of the unborn child (named Jude, the Patron Saint of Hopeless Cases and Impossible Tasks, is the narrator of the book) decide to stay in Camden and take in the "Ways" until the evening's appointment. They meet two men on a porch playing chess, or *The Chess Game*. A king piece is missing. Throughout the story, the chess players, Ruby and Cliff, give them hints as to where the king or Wizard may be hidden on this bloomy day of the 16th of June.

A popular expression today is, "there are a lot of Moving Parts." Well, *The Chess Game* has a lot of "Moving Parts" on the chess board and, more importantly, on the decayed streets of once proud, prosperous, Victor RCA Phonograph, Nipper Dog, Camden. In contrast, across the Delaware River and in view is the high rising sparkling architecture of the downtown business district of Philadelphia, separated from Camden by a few minutes ride on the Benjamin Franklin Bridge. Callahan deftly captures- using Callahanisms magical language, parables, poems, prose and yes, song - the hopelessness of the poor, unemployed, maltreated, and mentally ill of the real people of the street. The downtrodden sometimes dressing and playing acting roles, waiting for the king, I mean The Wizard to make "Ways" right again. They wander the city streets all day and night without shoes, and in their costumes, funny hats, just trying to survive in the dead city of Camden. There is a lack of food but plenty of drugs and alcohol are the bread of life. They are just trying to find their ways. "Your Father, He made the world uneven. Is it the same in Heaven?" Some brave souls, often the spiritual caring, and fearless Clergy, have moved into the bowels of the inner City to help show The Way.

The Chess Game will illuminate the minds of people on both sides of our Culture Divide to better understand that no one has a monopoly on righteous thought on Social Justice in our Country. I believe, however, that most readers will agree with Mr. Callahan that much more must be done to solve the social injustice that exists for many people living side by side with prosperity.

Hopefully, Callahan's unique and wondrous writing style will be set forth in many more of his works beyond his initial Trilogy – *The Black Rose, The Fish Finder and The Chess Game*. I sense that a special novelist has arrived on stage.

- *Harry C. J. Himes, Esq., Himes Law Firm*

Harry C. J. Himes, A lawyer in private practice.

Over the past twenty-four hours, I went on a twelve-hour journey through the streets of Camden, NJ. My journey was courtesy of Kevin Callahan's third book of his trilogy, *The Chess Game*. The journey starts with a visual look of the City through the windows of Cooper Hospital. The journey is described through the eyes of the as yet unconfirmed child of Choker and Cresty. Choker and Cresty have come to the hospital for an ultrasound.

We are introduced to the chess game when our trio realizes that they are 12 hours early for their doctor's appointment. So, they leave the Hospital and take to the street to pass the time. They happen upon the game right across from the hospital. They are drawn into the game by the charming players who challenge them to find the missing King/Wizard piece. On their quest they tour the center of the city which takes them step by step to all the landmarks that are part of Camden's rich history. On their "ways", they encounter the everyday characters that roam the streets in "The City Invincible". It is a magical and mystical journey through a down trodden place.

While searching for the King/Wizard, they also explore their individual faith journey through the songs of U2 and poems of Walt Whitman. The tale is a personal homage to anyone who has walked those streets. They have names and they have history. Real people live in those homes and they work every day "to rise up" and become the best that they and Camden can become.

Thanks Kevin, for a great story about a City that so many of us love!!
  - *Nancy Jerome, Board Member for Guadalupe Family Services and Long-time volunteer in the Forbidden Territory (North Camden)*

THE CHESS GAME

Table of Contents

Prologue	xv
Chapter 1	1
Chapter 2	33
Chapter 3	49
Chapter 4	63
Chapter 5	81
Chapter 6	99
Chapter 7	117
Chapter 8	133
Chapter 9	153
Chapter 10	169
Chapter 11	183
Chapter 12	195
Chapter 13	211
Chapter 14	229
Chapter 15	245
Chapter 16	261
Chapter 17	273
Chapter 18	289

THE CHESS GAME

Prologue

Today is the third part of a trilogy.

The first book, *The Black Rose*, which is set in Sea Isle and Avalon, takes place over four years from 2012 to 2016. The second book, *The Fish Finder*, which is set in Cape May, takes place over three months in 2015 during The Black Rose.

The Chess Game, the last book of *The Rose Finder Game* trilogy, takes place over one day – June 16, 2015 – in Camden.

In *The Fish Finder*, the main character of *The Black Rose*, Pete, is the narrator and he follows the lives of the other two main characters from the first book – his daughter, Andie, and her boyfriend, Byrd – during a summer job working with the potentate - an arborist, Marion, trimming trees in historic Cape May, trying to ease his guilt of being a former abortion doctor.

Andie and Byrd are also trying to forget their past and move on from the death of Pete in *The Black Rose* by changing their names to Cresty and Choker, and taking up surfing and judo, respectively, instead of playing pickup basketball. They both have dropped out of Ursinus College.

On this day - a *"blooming* day to be alive," as Cliff says today during his game of chess with

Ruby – both Cresty and Choker are looking at their future... and a fuzzy photograph of me.

I'm looking at them with blatant obsequiousness, (Yeah, although I'm an unborn baby I can show off, too).

THE CHESS GAME

Chapter 1

Without the benefit of being born yet, I've never received any advice and so have never thought about life, or living. I just listen and observe. I don't believe the view is a detriment in the least.

My mother is scheduled today for an ultrasound, but really I'm the one being checked out. So, I do feel, at least for this day, that it is proper and fair to see my outside world through her eyes and mine.

There is so much to learn, I know. I've been around for almost three weeks now and from Day One, I've been listening. I see and hear and, so I learn from the outsiders. I also feel.

There are many moving parts out there in the world's cocoon. Everyone seemingly has a role while some follow their paths. I will say, it seems, the wanderers and the seekers are only permitted, or choose, to move in certain ways in their own spaces of life.

My observation is simple: the people out there walking around in this world are always looking to protect themselves first; If they can, they will move to attack for their advantage. I see this, as if their existence is a calculated game of expertise and experience… and just plan chance. Or Rochambeau as Cresty says.

If life weren't so serious, each day could be a joyous game filled with songs.

My morning's view out of this hospital window shows me a new world in an old city.

At first glance, a block and a half down the street, two men sit rigid at a table that is centered on a slumping porch.

After deliberate thought, one man slides a piece on a board.

Reactively, the other man swipes all the other pieces off the black and white checkered board and on the floor scattered around his red shoes.

The man in the waiting room on the seventh floor with my mother is my father. He puts his phone up against the window. He snaps a photograph of Camden with Philadelphia in the background.

Looking straight ahead, the city consists of mostly old, decrepit buildings mixed between weeded empty lots and rising new structures, some with only freshly welded steel showing. Towering over all, in the center of the city, stands a majestic grayish-white concrete structure. This wide building at the base and first seven floors or so rises into a tower with a clock right below the

THE CHESS GAME

spiral top. The two red hands on the stone face say its seven o'clock. Perhaps the clock hasn't been moved ahead yet for daylight savings time? My father's phone says its 8 o'clock.

A cop on a horse faces the street with the tower behind him. A man without shoes holds a trash can lid his left arm and points a trash-picking metal pole at the tower. He sits on a police barricade like a wooden horse.

To the right of the tower, but not as high as it, rises a modern building with long vertical windows systematically placed, like for rooms, with a big red letter "R" stretching from the roof down the brick side for two floors.

To the left, rises a building of yellowish-brown brick, an odd color. This solid fortress-like building is much more modern than the clock tower. It is new, like the "R" building, and both buildings are the same height. The top floors of both buildings are on the same level as my view out the hospital window. But the fortress-like building only has slender horizontal slots for windows and not large glass openings like the "R" building.

I think, if you could string a wire from the top floor of each building connecting all three structures – the hospital, the solid fortress and the "R" building - a circus clown on a tightrope could walk evenly from one building to the next. His balance bar would not be obstructed by any other buildings as high these three structures and the sky walker would be far enough away from the tower as not to touch it with his pole.

The way I see this view, the brave tightrope walker wouldn't want to look down. No, he would want to keep his eyes straight ahead.

He wouldn't want to look up at the clock tower structure either. He probably would lose his balance trying to tilt and see the pointed peak, a bit like the Empire State Building, but without its obvious height. Still, it would be hard, or more accurately a challenge, to keep his eyes off of the old gray City Hall building with its wide base and pointed clock tower. The attraction would almost be magnetic.

Once on top of the "R" building, now beyond the Coke-bottle shaped building with the tardy clock, the daredevil would then turn his focus to the wire leading to the yellowish-brown brick building. He might feel scared. He wouldn't want to fall.

No, he wouldn't want to topple against the walls of the yellowish-brown brick building. The barbed wired tops would surely cut him badly. He wouldn't want to fall inside the walls either. No,

THE CHESS GAME

the concrete courtyard of that Camden prison has been stained with enough blood.

However, from there, the tight-roper could look back right into my own enclosed window here at the Cooper Hospital, a building which sits in the middle of a city housing America's poorest people along with the country's highest crime rate.

He would see clear glass. The glass is perfect. The tint is dark enough to shield the early morning sun, but clear enough to let you know this mid-June day is going to be cook a hot dog on the curb hot.

I wonder if the clear glass is tinted enough for the tight-roper to see his reflection? Perhaps within the last 15-foot stretch or so, "a foul shot away," as Choker and Cresty would say from their basketball playing days… which ended last year in college.

But, I reason, a tight-roper wouldn't be able to see into all the windows of all three buildings attached by my imaginary wire. He wouldn't see all the brazen hope and broken dreams living so close together in the city, connected as if by an umbilical cord.

He wouldn't be able to see the dreams and sheltered lives in the "R" building with wide windows.

He wouldn't be able to see the dreams and shattered lives in the Camden jail either with its slotted windows.

He wouldn't be able to see the hopeful new lives sharing floors with the regretful nuanced lives here in Cooper Hospital.

He wouldn't be able to see me.

I wonder, is the one-way view fair?

Also, I wonder what the tight-roper would see into the windows of City Hall. But I realize the tower windows are either dark-tinted or the curtains are closed.

I know the cop on the horse facing the street can't see into the tower behind him, but surely feels its height over him. The man without shoes, sitting on a wooden police barricade like a horse, holding a trash can lid and pointing a trash-picking metal pole at the tower sure seems like he can see behind the curtains.

The tower, pointed toward the clouds that drift toward the east from the wind off the river, stares at them both.

Looking beyond the city to the west, toward the rest of waking America, under nauseous skies, over waves of pain and a halcyon history, the tight roper would first see the sturdy steel of an impressive suspension bridge built during the Industrial

THE CHESS GAME

Revolution. The rusting blue mountain of a bridge is magnificent in size and structure. The alabaster city on the other side of the river dwarfs the purple-pained city on this side of the bridge.

But a tight-roper wouldn't be here in Camden looking at Philadelphia. He would only be looking at the wire and what it is connected to ahead. He would see just his single path and his lone possibility.

Looking behind the hospital, the tight-roper would see green to the east. He would see the green tops of the trees in suburban South Jersey… mixed in between the blacktopped parking lots of the overflowing shopping and strip malls. But, again, he would only be looking at the wire and what his bare feet connect to ahead.

From the hospital window, looking south, the high-wire dancer could see the other hospital in Camden, a hospital with the towering statue of the Blessed Mother. He might be looking, or at least sneaking peaks, at Mother Mary, when his balance feels off, when he is tilting toward a splattering below in the street.

The aerial acrobat might even see a leaf wafting aimlessly beneath the holy statute, into a restful patch of grass and out of view.

Leaves and grass… below Our Lady of Lourdes Hospital… where the sick and dying people go… the ones who believe in prayer, well, at least, Choker said so on the ride north here from the Jersey Shore.

Looking ahead, with a swift peek below, the tight-roper would see the one man flipping the thick book on his lap closed and reactively picking up the pieces scattered around the red shoes.

When Cresty heard the time of her girl, well, woman's doctor's appointment, she typed in "8 a.m. on June 16, 2015" on her iPhone. I do remember. I was already almost three weeks old that day. Now, you would think there isn't much to remember when you aren't even a month old, but there is so much…

Every breath. Every second. Each beat.

Every of everything is your life you know.

Each tick is your best heartbeat ever with the next one promising to be even better. And you already know so much since your lunchbox of life is already packed with knowledge, a suitcase so to speak for the journey. A suitcase some people open, and others keep shut.

So, without a gym bag for a change of clothes, but with plenty of luggage, Choker and Cresty hustled from Cape May to Camden for the 8 a.m.

appointment with Dr. Burk, "the best gyno specialist around," her father Pete told her as a kid, "and a left-handed hitting catcher who can slap line drives to the opposite field."

Choker playfully shakes Cresty when the receptionist at Dr. Burk's office tells us the appointment isn't until 8 P.M – tonight!

Cresty shakes him back, but stirs him harder, as if saying this is for real, as the other nurse-types in the hospital office sip their second cup of morning coffee.

There is nothing to do… but "take a wander, inhale Camden," Choker determines while heartily hugging Cresty and me, "just like Pete would do."

Humming at first, Choker starts to sing U2's Angel of Harlem. He turns to her and blares, "You could be the Angel of *Camden*."

We don't wander even a full block. We stop at the house with the two older guys at the checkered table on the porch… and half of them or so still on the floor.

The men look up slowly. Deliberately. They stare at Choker, who is wearing a red number seven t-shirt with black letters.

"Lucky number seven?" the man with the red shoes says with an open mouth revealing just three teeth.

"You know the Biblical meaning of the number seven?" the other man, the one closest with pieces in his hand, says without turning around. "Seven is God's word. He reveals the number over 50 times in the opening, The Book of Revelation, and more than 700 total times, intentionally, in the bible."

"Actually, sirs, I just wear number seven because it was the jersey number of Pistol Pete, well when he was with the Celtics," Choker says apologetically. "He wore number 44 with the Jazz and in college, but he chose number seven for his last team... for some reason."

Cresty adds, "The Edge wears the Number seven jersey, too, but the U2 guitarist says he just likes the look and there is no hidden meaning. If anyone would be spreading the biblical meaning of number seven, though, it would be U2.

"The Irish band is full of subtle Christian messages."

"Amen," says the man farthest away with his mouth closed as he kisses each piece before placing it on a square.

The two elderly men resume hunching over the wooden table with shaky legs. They stare at the table. Neither says anything.

THE CHESS GAME

The two guys at the table rest their elbows on their knees. They must be in their 70's. Perhaps older.

They are playing chess. No moves are made yet.

The one man facing us rests his elbows on the table and under his chin. He takes off his pinstripe blue railroad engineer hat and places it on the tilted table.

"Cliff, here, thinks he is going to win this game," he says smiling as noticeable as his red shoes, showing off one upper tooth and two lower teeth. "This, he thinks, is his day to beat Ruby."

With his lips still tense, the other man laughs, saying "A *blooming* day to be alive."

"*Blooming* don't matter a blooming bit to Ruby," the three-tooth smiling man declares.

"No. It doesn't. You start every game knocking off the pieces," the other man says in a steady tone that would suggest neither anger nor approval.

"Cliffy, that's just the way we've played for seventy years, since we were seven years old and neighbors here," Ruby says as if upset that he needs to send a reminder. "That's just the *ways* Ruby plays."

"I know, makes for quite lugubrious games," Cliff says. "Don't change your *ways*. But back as kids, back then you played with a king."

"Lost it."

"Lost it?" More like hid it," Cliff says, turning around and looking up at us with a gentle smile. He has all his teeth above a sturdy jaw and tight cheeks. "Ruby said I would never capture his king again after I won every game as kids. So, one day, young Rudy, now I call him Ruby, got on his red bike he hid his king, the black one, somewhere in Camden."

"He's not the king," Ruby says pounding the table and laughing riotously. "He'd be the Wizard."

"He hid the king ... the Wizard, somewhere, he says," Cliff continues. "The piece is somewhere public, somewhere in view, and somewhere important in the city, so he says. But I never found it and I walked all over the city ... even back to my home in Fairview all the way down in South Camden from his house here. In Center City."

Around this chess game without a king, the city's chaos spills out methodically onto the streets. Juiced-up doctors hustle from the parking garage to the hospital for their morning shifts. Sleepy nurses stumble back to their cars after their endless all-nighters. A hot dog vendor leans up against a street sign pole without a sign.

The street chef sends steam into the already thick air every time he opens the lid over the

THE CHESS GAME

boiling water while he yells, "Get yer *baddest ass* breakfast dogs here."

"Mind if we watch?" Cresty asks with a fascinated interest, looking at the chessboard. "We have a whole day to kill."

"You'd did come to the right place if you want to see a killing," Ruby laughs mightily, which shakes both straps on his dungaree overalls down his bony and bare shoulders. "Maybe a deuce. You'd see me beat old Cliffy and you'd might just see a shoot out on the corner. There'd not been a murder in two whole days. Maybe a deuce and a half."

An ambulance siren screams by us like "dang lightnin' on fire," as Ruby says. Another siren whistles by us going in the other direction. We lean against the splintered blue and tan rail of the porch, knocking off some paint chips, and absorb all the "Cacophony of Camden," as Cliff says. Ruby flips up his shoulder straps like he is going to battle in this chess game that hadn't started.

The men stare at the board as if they can move the pieces with their minds, their will.

"Come eat an egg, cheese and doggie sandwich… they will be just thinking what to do if the one makes this move or if the other makes that move," barks the hot dog vendor at us from across the street and below a puff of steam. He is wearing a faded purple Camden High basketball jersey. He slumps with his back against the sign-less street sign. His belly bulge is surrounded by the steam. "Yes they do. They play the game on a higher level."

"You want the best damn breakfast dog this side of the river... you got the best damn breakfast dog this side of the river."

They must play on a higher level since Ruby *really* doesn't have a king in front of him. The space is empty.

A doctor with perfect black hair parted high on the side shuffles up the porch steps with the heads of the nails needing to be smashed down. He is dressed in his all-white smock and loose greenish pants with the front rope, or string, untied and flapping. He looks wildly tired, weary even though his hair doesn't move. He stumbles inside the row home, twirls and plops on a sofa near the open window facing the porch. There is no breeze to fan the straight rising steam from the hot dog vendor. He is sweating more than us.

"Good luck beating old Rube today Cliffmaster," the doc garbles.

With a swipe of his right arm, the man with three teeth knocks over all the chess pieces.

THE CHESS GAME

The two players quietly pick up the chess pieces. The doc hands a pawn that flew through the window to Cliff.

With the pieces piled on the table, Ruby taps the empty space where the black king should be.

"Find the king yet?" the Doc asks aloud, but to no one in particular.

"He'd be the Wizard," Ruby says, gnashing his three teeth. "I don't know any kings. Dang, there'd be just one king in is this city."

The white king is set first by Cliff on the bumpy board. From up close, we see the uneven checkered board leans a bit to the left side.

"The President is in place," the soft-spoken Cliff says. As he reaches for the table the short sleeves of his wrinkle-free white t-shirt inch up to reveal his rock solid biceps and his strong lower shoulders, his side delts. "The piece is the Prospector of Peace."

He places his white queen.

"Her Majesty's Ship," Cliff says in a deep and declarative voice.

The black queen is placed by Ruby. The piece wobbles on the bumpy square.

"The Lady," Ruby says.

The bishops, knights and rooks are placed one-by-one in order by the two men, always the white pieces first and then the black ones.

The two men at the table bow their heads as if they are saying a prayer. Cliff finishes first. He stares at the pieces on the board as a third siren screams by us and sails into the city. As if on cue, or in a video game, a fourth siren wails back toward the hospital. With one arm and then one leg at a time, the doctor awkwardly climbs through the window.

The crazed doc jams his outstretched right hand on the board for balance and four white pills spill out of his smock's breast pocket and onto the board. In one motion, Ruby swipes up all the pills without disturbing one chess piece on the slanted board. He then places the four pills on the space where his king should be.

A Camden County police car, lights flashing and with sirens blaring, screams by the porch as the doctor stumbles down the steps, cursing the protruding nail heads, stops on the chipped curb and reaches into his top pocket. He looks into the pocket for a minute or so before stumbling up the steps, plopping back inside again and pulling off the cushions on the sofa. After five minutes and no moves in the chess game, he launches himself

THE CHESS GAME

outside and sits on a fire hydrant with its cap hanging by a chain near the steps. His lime green pants match the dry fire hydrant.

The parking garage attendant, wearing yellow shorts and an unbuttoned red-flowered Hawaiian shirt that matches his thin reddish-gray goatee, hands the doctor half of his breakfast sandwich from the vendor as he helps him across Benson Street. Moments later, the doctor weaves a black Range Rover onto the street, scraping the sign-less parking garage sign that was behind the street vendor's cart, but the man had moved his *baddest ass* breakfast dogs mobile a few feet away. The vendor moves the cart back against the bare sign pole as Doc weaves down the street.

"Doc will be right back again," says the parking garage attendant. "Doctor Knight knows driving ain't right… right now."

"I know," Cliff says. "When you go off his shift he moves his fancy wheels on the street so he doesn't have to pay for parking."

"He knows how to play," the parking garage says while stroking his thin reddish-gray goatee, as if adding emphasis, "Doc, yeah, he knows how to play… the game."

"Say, when can I get in on the game here?" he quickly adds, tugging on his Hawaiian shirt.

"When you learn the right people," Ruby says.

"I'll learn," the parking attendant says in an unconvincing burst. "And when I do, when I do… I will be sure to learn my kid… to learn his kids… how to play… how to play the chess game."

"The Game of Chess," Ruby says, reaching over with his skinny arms and tugging on the attendant's flashy shirt. "The Game of Chess to those who don't play."

"Teach me, too" Cresty says, rather pleads. "I think I want to learn."

"You want to play?" Cliff asks sternly. "Study first. Then play. Study the mistakes and learn from the mistakes. Then play."

"I will," she says with dripping determination like the streaking sweat on her forehead.

"Just let us know when you are ready to play then," says Cliff as his glasses start to fog up in the humidity, shielding the bottom of his eyes like a mask.

"I'd learned how'd to play," Ruby says proudly, pulling tight his shoulder straps. "I'd learned by just watchin'. And now sweet Ruby can't be beatin'."

"Me too," Doc says appearing mysteriously, like from out of the steam, walking steadily up the steps. "Just watch and learn. The times aren't a changin'. He stumbles on the top step and curses the nail heads.

"Study the board," the doc adds when done swearing. "Study the board like a... like a Geandekeen experiment... think how to think."

The checkered chessboard is bumpy. There are various sized holes, but all divots are small on the board. The four sides aren't even close to being even. The playing surface is a grayish rock. The squares are scratched in opposite directions, delineating for black and white spaces.

"The board is made of pumice," Cliff says, adjusting his seat after sliding the thick red book that matches the color of Ruby's sneakers from his lap to underneath him.

Waiting for Ruby to make a move, he pulls out and opens the red book with blocked yellow letters on the cover "MANDARIN."

Cliff reads a few words, using his right index finger, and then writes a symbol on a yellow legal pad with faded green lines.

"Mandarin is the predominant language in China," he says, looking up to see if Ruby has moved yet. "It developed during the reign of the Jin Dynasty, almost a thousand years ago, when the Mongols built a large wall to stop invasions."

"Did it work?" Cresty asks. "The wall?"

"Does a wall work? Cliff asks before quickly continuing, "The language has lasted, but the Jin dynasty endured only a thousand years, into the middle of the 13th century.

"So, the answer is relative. The Great Wall didn't work. It was the last dynasty before the invasion of the Mongols and Kublai Khan."

Cliff is wearing pressed gray slacks and polished black shoes. His white t-shirt is tucked under a black belt with a shiny square buckle. The belt pulls in his waist, making his V-shaped upper body look even more powerful. He is a small man, but when Cresty asked him how he stays so "fookin fit" he just said, "got fit first" and that he worked construction… "as a loyal laborer."

"Yeah, but his muscles can't beat old Rube in the Game of Chess," Ruby tells us. "Cliff is a grad of Penn… worked 44 years in construction after returning from the Navy… went to classes across the river at night… learned dang words like lugubrious while old Rube learned… learned to play his lonely guitar at night… Cliffy graduated at 66… now reads and talks Chinese in between moves, delayin' Rube… but he don't know how to play Ruby's guitar… no one does."

"Erudite knowledge is the most satisfying," Cliff smiles.

THE CHESS GAME

"Nope... he still can't beat sweet Ruby... he can never capture the Wizard."

"Hey, why don't you two go look for his king, Ruby's Wizard, for me?" Cliff pleads. "Ruby says the piece is hidden in the city somewhere."

Rolling up the bottom of his blue overalls, showing off his sparkling red high-top sneakers, Ruby pulls out his heralded guitar with three strings from the side of his rocking chair. He strums and sings, "Only The Wizard, can fix everything."

Closing gently his book, Cliff tells us Ruby was the dump truck driver for the construction outfit where they worked together. "Drove up until a few years ago," and then adding, "Ask Ruby to play his three-string guitar, the same one he played in the truck."

Ruby strums and sings, "Only The Wizard, can fix everything... in The Game of Chess."

"Ruby used to sing all of Elvis' songs in the truck," Cliff says. "Ruby loved The King... except he didn't know the words to the songs... he made up his own words... like The Game of Chess instead of The Chess Game."

Choker and Cresty look at each other and both say, "The King... like The Fish Finder."

"Where is mighty Ruby's guitar?" Ruby asks

with his guitar on his lap below the checkered table.

"Here somewhere ... has to be ... Ruby lives here at the same house here on Benson Street where he grew up and old," Cliff says without judgment. "He calls his porch, the Porch of Versailles. Isn't that funny?"

"Well, Ruby, a sweet and mighty as he is, old Rube is not a king, so don't have a palace, just a porch, so this is my Versailles," Ruby says. "Ruby will give you a hint where to find the Wizard: The king bridges the people."

We make our move... to leave.

Cliffs says he will call on Ruby's cell phone if he has any more hints for us.

"We'll make sure you are all right and alive," he says as Cresty brushes paint chips from her gray cutoff sweat pants.

"Perhaps, maybe you should fear a homeless looking man pushing a shopping cart and wearing an Abe Lincoln black stovepipe top hat," Ruby warns. "Old Rube thinks so."

"He is also looking for the chess piece behind his mirror sunglasses," Cliff says. "He's been looking for the Wizard for years. He's been looking to breach the bourgeois forever."

Ruby says, "There could be, will be others. Be

careful, you be."

"Careful," Cliff huffs. "You mean careless… in this city… careless political corruption is our history, our story of Camden."

"Come on now Cliff," Ruby says. "Only three of our former mayors were locked up… only Angelo Errichetti, Arnold Webster and Milton Milan… and in that order."

"And the city has suffered at their hands," Cliff says. "Still suffering, I'd say.

"In 2012, in cities with over 50,000 residents Camden was number one for violent crime per capita."

"Perhaps," Ruby says. "But Ruby says the people are trying. That year, over 1,100 guns were turned over to local churches.

"And the lawmen are better, a new police department was formed this year. Ruby doesn't know what The Year of 2014 will be remembered as in your Mandarin Chinese book, but in our city, it is the year the Camden County Police Department took over, took control. Took command like me in chess. That's good."

"Good? Like your chess strategy?" Cliff laughs. "Ruby uses the French Defense always.

"Always, following my lead of e4, he employs e6. I must admit the opening always gives me counterattacking opportunities on the side of his, the queen, forcing him to work the side of his missing king."

"You mean The Wizard," Cresty says playfully.

"What is e4 and e6?" Choker asks, not minding he is confused, and then adding, "Anything like $E=Mc2$, like The Fish Finder preaches?"

"The game of chess is played on a board of eight rows, or ranks, marked by numbers one to eight, and eight columns, or files, noted by the letters a to h," Cliff says. "So, each of the pieces have a letter, like Q for queen, except the pawn. So e4 means the pawn moves to the e4 square."

"Simple," Ruby says. "Got it?"

"Got it," Choker replies while tapping the side of his head. "Simple like Ruby's guitar."

Bouncing down the steps, Choker and Cresty walk away along with the parking attendant, who pulls a bottle in a brown bag from inside his yellow shorts. The flapping baggy Hawaiian shirt covered the bottle. He hands the bag to Choker, who fakes a swig.

"Come back when you find the Wizard," Ruby screams, adding a haunting laugh.

"I'll be back," Choker screams and then sings silly like, "We'll be back Mr. Ruby… even if its not til Tuesday."

THE CHESS GAME

Where?

Choker and Cresty walk back up Benson Street toward the hospital. We don't know where to go. We look up and see the clock on the tower. We are pulled there. We go there.

There is a grass park with a crossing concrete sidewalk in front of City Hall. Across the street is the PATCO Speedline, which crosses the Ben Franklin Bridge and connects the endless suburbia of South Jersey in front of us to Philadelphia behind us in the west. The flaking red metal staircase of the PATCO station dips below the corner of Market and Fifth Streets. A few yards from the descending steps stands a red brick building surrounded by young people, six or seven, huddled and smoking wrinkled cigarettes. This popular building was a former chain drug store. It is now a methadone clinic.

"Says here City Hall is the tallest building in Camden," Choker says, reading his iPhone. "The original City Hall was on the corner of Benson and Haddon Avenue where Cooper Hospital is now."

"Down the street from the chess game," Cresty adds. "Look, the South tower is engraved with 'IN A DREAM I SAW A CITY INVINCIBLE.'"

"That's an excerpt from a Walt Whitman poem," Choker reads from his phone.

"The front is engraved with 'NO LEGACY IS SO RICH AS HONESTY,'" Cresty reads from the four-story block building below the tower.

"That's from William Shakespeare's 'All's Well that Ends Well,'" Choker reads off his phone.

Halting his reading, the phone rings. Chiming church bells startle a pack of the Methadonians. Cliff is calling already on Choker's cell.

"We're at City Hall, I can read another inscription," Cresty says, grabbing his phone and walking up the wide center steps. "The engraving says, 'WHERE THERE IS NO VISION THE PEOPLE PERISH - PROVERBS 29:18.'"

"The Navy's baby, the USS Indianapolis perished," Cliff injects. "First the ship did the perishing... and then the treaty cruiser perished.

"What?" Cresty asks. "What you say."

"I say, she was built in Camden at the old New York Shipyard to swim like a dolphin can swim, to be a hero, to be the king... but she delivered the goods for the first atom bomb to an air base in the South Pacific. Four days later she was torpedoed by the Japanese and sunk in 12 minutes, taking 300 crewmen to the bottom while the other 900 spent four days floating in the ocean... about 600 were shark bait... the other 300 were finally, well eventually rescued.

THE CHESS GAME

"To this day, the deliverance is the largest loss of life... at sea by the Navy.

"The chess game... the board, though... survived."

We wander over to the corner, across from City Hall, in front of the methadone clinic building that was a Rite Aid drug store, which is now a meeting place, like a town hall. More Methadonians are hanging outside, smoking curled-up cigarettes and saying stuff like "I'm no dumbass bitch" and "keep the line straighter so I can get inside quicker."

Cliff continues: "The chess set was bought by my father while stationed in the Mariana Islands, which is an archipelago that rose from volcanoes on the ocean floor. The pumice is hardened lava. Pumice floats. Pumice lives unattached. Attached to a rock, pumice sinks.

"While clinging on the side of a raft, at first no one wanted to play my father. He played alone... that was that. But the game took my dad's mind from worrying about survival. So he played the chess game.

"After one day, with their shipmates being eaten around them, other sailors wanted to play. My dad let them, one at a time ... he was a hero... just for one day"

Looking north, across Market Street, stands a 15-foot, old-fashioned street clock a few feet from the corner. We wait a few minutes, realizing the clock is stuck on 10:10. A guy under the clock is selling used photos of former Hollywood stars. Samba music with horns and a circular whistling sound beats from a portable CD player on a leaning card table with a buckled front leg. Cresty recognizes the song but can't …

"What's up with the clock?" Choker suddenly asks, breaking Cresty's thought while nodding to the frozen clock behind the man, who doesn't answer. He stares, as if in a trance, straight ahead as Choker asks again, "What's up with the clock?"

"What you'd say… fitting, I'd say."

The man spins from behind the table. He is sitting on a motorized mini-scooter. A toy cannon, like the ones used in the Civil War with the oversized wooden wheels, is mounted between his legs on the seat and pointed toward two Methadonians parked in a car swearing at the clock.

"Shhhh with the cussin," the cannon man hushes and then says to us, "Mornin'… my name is Mornie… I'd used to be a jockey before Garden State Park racetrack in Cherry Hill shuttered… I'd say, 10:10 is the moment Abraham Lincoln was

THE CHESS GAME

shot.

"Like the clock, Camden be stuck in time."

"Not us," Cresty says, pulling up Choker's arm to keep wandering, to go somewhere.

A man shielded by mirror sunglasses pushing an empty shopping clock turns the corner and almost whacks us. He is wearing a tan LL Bean vest jacket with a green stripped-sleeve turtleneck and an Abe Lincoln black stovepipe top hat. The wheels on the shopping cart whistle away from us, squeaking as he whispers something about "forever and ever" and then loudly warns, "don't try to be heroes," with his back to us so we can't see our reflection off his mirror sunglasses.

Mornie pivots, pointing the cannon on the front of the seat of the motorized mini-scooter at the shopping cart man.

"You're a miracle," Mornie says turning back to us, his eyes only reaching Cresty's belly. "Just like the stars on Hollywood Boulevard... you're a miracle if you survive the streets of Camden... if you survive, you're a miracle... I swear to you."

We look up at the clock on City Hall. Choker checks his iPhone. The tower clock is an hour behind real time... but not stuck on 10:10.

Walking north toward the bridge, Choker and Cresty hold hands at the Tabernacle Faith Church on the corner of Fifth and Cooper Streets. The church faces the Rutgers University Early Learning Research Academy. A Rutgers-Camden student on the corner is playing a six-string guitar and singing a U2 song. There is an empty bucket in front of him.

On the other side of the street, on the corner of Fourth and Cooper, is the United States Courthouse and Post Office. The four-story concrete building is next to a brownstone church. Saint Paul Episcopal Church looks like a stone fort.

The concrete of City Hall and the U.S. Courthouse is the same ashen color of the pumice chess set. There are no holes in the concrete, though, like on the board and in the pieces. Can the buildings float?

Choker begins singing with the Rutgers-Camden student busking on the corner to U2's "I Still Haven't Found What I'm Looking For." Like Ruby, Choker starts making up his own words again with emphasis:

> I have *drowned in their fountains*
> I have run with *shields*
> Only to be *without do*
> Only to be *without do*
> I have *shun*, I have *wailed*

THE CHESS GAME

I have scaled city *hall*
Said it was
Only to be *without do*
So, I still *won't be bound without keeping score*
So, I still *won't be bound without keeping score*

Choker flips over the empty bucket and balances on the rocking edge. A quarter rolls around the bucket as he continues singing:

I believe in *Camden* come
When all the *races be seething* as one
Seething as one
Yes, I'm still *dreaming*
He broke the *clowns*, he loosed *their reigns*
Carried the cross of *their game*
Stoke me sane
Yo bro I believed it
So, I still *won't be bound without keeping score*
So, I still *won't be bound without keeping score*
So, I still *won't be bound without keeping score*
So, I still *won't be bound without keeping score*

Choker flips over the bucket and drops in five single dollars, telling the college kid *"he saved it on parking since the hospital has free parking for patients."*

"I knew you had to be sick," the college kid says. "Why else would you be here ... unless you go to school here, too?"

"We're looking for the King," Choker says.

"You mean," Cresty says, "The Wizard."

THE CHESS GAME

Chapter 2

The melodic, soothing lyrics from the college street singer drift onto the city campus with us. Choker and Cresty wander over the train tracks on the edge of this New Jersey state university, looking back at an advertisement on the rattling River Line. The ad for the hometown college is the length of two trolley cars. We admire a row of refurbished brownstone buildings, including a couple of fraternity houses, on Cooper Street, the southern border of the urban campus.

A smell of cooked bacon from another street vendor swirls in the air along with a tinge of excitement from Choker and Cresty. And fear. I sense them both. Truthfully, excitement and fear don't feel much different.

"I still haven't found what I'm looking for," Choker sings as he skips off the hard brick-designed sidewalk and onto the comfortable grassy grounds of Rutgers where the dead winter leaves mix with the rising summer strands of grass.

We crossed into this oasis from where there was an emptiness and quietness on the city streets, from where the lonely sidewalks were repaved as a result of the various revival attempts downtown. We watched and listened to the energy and buzzing of young people walking with a purpose to their classes. Or to somewhere else. Perhaps somewhere other than the half empty city streets.

The desolate patches of downtown don't mesh for a city with so much history and so close to Philadelphia.

A man with a ragged beard wearing a spiffy blue suit weaves in front of us on the brick sidewalk. He thoughtlessly lifts up his right arm and flicks a tree branch. The morning dew sprays us. He turns backwards, fumbling with his satchel a bit, and mouths the word "sorry" but with no sound.

Choker doesn't seem uncomfortable at all walking the streets with Cresty. Maybe he is at ease because he is big and athletic. He stands 6-foot-2. He is a solid 185 pounds despite not playing basketball over the past winter for the first time since his shot finally reached the six-foot basket in the driveway… the hoop hung by his dad at their rich North Jersey home.

Maybe he is so relaxed because Cresty is so confident. And she is also athletic looking still with defined shoulder and upper back muscles like Cliff. She didn't play basketball either this year after taking off from college. She didn't return to Ursinus for her sophomore year after her dad,

THE CHESS GAME

Pete... went missing. But she still wears her basketball sneakers with the letters P E T E printed neatly on both heels, and tied tightly.

Choker knows she could handle herself if grabbed by an unknowing street person or even a mugger.

But still, as Mornie, the man under the frozen clock stuck on 10:10 said, "this is Camden... Camden. New Jersey."

They stop. We stop. We look up as if the acrobat on the tightrope is up there above and will tell us where to go, will warn us if the angry man in the Able Lincoln hat will ram us with the shopping cart. Instead, the bright yellow ledges with spotlights on the Victor Tower and its stained-glass windows of Nipper the Dog on each side gains our full attention. The refurbished tower is behind us, close to the river that I have never seen... well except from the hospital window.

We really don't know which way to go. How should we? Make a left toward the river? Go straight toward the rusting blue Ben Franklin Bridge connecting Camden and Philadelphia? Stay inside the safety of Rutgers' guarded campus? Could the king be here?

They look behind them and see a 7-11 tucked in a nook on Cooper Street. We didn't notice the store when we passed it because we were just killing time. We walk over to the convenience store. Cresty buys a bag of chocolate M&Ms and a bag of peanut M&Ms. She mixes the two bags into a larger plastic green 7-11 bag as we wander over to the bacon-smelling silver street vending cart with rusty wheels and a red sign on top that promotes "Fresh Fruit Salad." Choker buys two bacon and egg sandwiches from the skinny street vendor wearing a Woodrow Wilson High orange t-shirt, saying "breakfast good enough for the college kids is good enough for us dropouts."

We look east toward the haze of the rising sun and see a new Barnes & Noble on the corner of Broadway and Cooper. Looking beyond the bookstore with the empty coffee shop, we can see the 676 Interstate that leads from the bridge to the leafy suburbs of South Jersey. Where 676 curves south, there is a rusting white-water tower on top of five-story, brown brick building. Is water inside? Is the water rusty?

"The water was used to put out fires, not to drink," Choker says aloud, as if the thought just floated from his mind to his tongue.

"I know you're not dumb," Cresty says. "You don't have to show off your knowledge. None of the college kids will hear you... and none of them

THE CHESS GAME

would care you went to a prestigious high school like them.

"You don't sound as smart as Cliff though."

"Yup. He's *erudite* smar*t,*" Choker says. "I don't know what that even means... I guess I could learn."

The angry middle-aged man wearing a tan L. L. Bean vest jacket with a green stripped-sleeve turtleneck darts out from under the 676 overpass. He is wearing mirror sunglasses coming out of the shadow. With both hands, he points up toward the hospital from where we started this morning and then simultaneously, with hands outstretched in each direction, he points to the big red-letter R on the Rutgers dormitory tower on our left and then swings both arms to point to the yellowish-brown brick jail to our right.

Then, with arms crossed over the L. L. Bean vest, he stares, seemingly studies the clock on the City Hall tower, which says its 8:06... but is an hour behind.

He walks backwards, dipping his head so the Abe Lincoln black stovepipe top hat clears the overpass and he pulls out the shopping cart with squeaky wheels. He charges. He pushes the cart towards us, then stops just across the street and leans on the empty silver cart.

From inside his vest he pulls out a brown cardboard sign with red letters. The creased sign reads: "The Wizard will fix everything."

A freshly washed white shuttle bus with the words "CAMDEN RISING" in black letters blocks shields Choker from walking across the street to the homeless looking man with the empty shopping cart and mirror sunglasses.

The man is gone.

We wander up the block a bit to look for him, peeking into the darkness under the bridge but not stepping into its shadow.

Between the City Hall clock tower building and the B&N bookstore spreads the campus of the LEAP Academy, a private learning center. Kids are doing kid stuff in the playground in the shadow of the Route 30 underpass and the overpass for 10th Street, which leads into North Camden.

A basketball sails over the fence and rolls to Choker, who is still standing on the corner pivoting his head while looking for the man with the Wizard sign. Choker takes a few dribbles, then makes a crossover dribble move and in one smooth motion flings a two-handed chest pass over the fence.

Although dressed in cargo hiking pants with thick-soled hiking boots and the tight red t-shirt with the black number seven, Choker looks like he could walk onto the LEAP playground and dunk the basketball.

"Nice to finally see you pass the ball," says Cresty, poking him.

She hesitates while pulling off a hooded gray Ursinus College sweatshirt, revealing a baggy, crusty green Number 24 jersey with the sleeves cut off... which reveals her muscular shoulders. She unties her red hair that was balled up against the hood and allows the long strands to fall over the back of her cut triceps.

"That homeless looking dude wearing mirror sunglasses pushing the shopping cart won't mess with us now, not when he sees your double-barrel," Choker says, poking her back. He squeezes both of Cresty's biceps with his two hands. He hugs her. Us.

We turn back to the left and see a meter maid dressed in a tight-fitting blue uniform. She is writing a ticket while holding the hand of a young girl. Her preschool daughter?

Looking toward the river, we can't help but seeing, well comparing the smaller brick buildings of Camden in the forefront of the shiny glass skyscraping towers of center city Philadelphia. They reflect the sun back across the river like mirrors.

The information kiosk sign on campus tells us how Rutgers University–Camden is one of the three regional colleges of the main campus in New Brunswick. There is another site in Newark. Rutgers-Camden "is a research university," the sign boasts.

Choker's phone beeps. Cliff has sent a text titled "Secret Mission."

"Another hint?" Cresty asks. "Where do we start looking for the king? Or should we just pray?

"St. Anthony, St. Anthony please come around, something is lost and must be found."

The text reads:

> THE USS INDY BUILT HERE IN CAMDEN BOBBED AND WEAVED ACROSS THE WORLD TO TINIAN ISLAND ... ITS HULL FILLED WITH ENRICHED URANIUM ... PACKING ALMOST HALF OF THE URANIUM-235 IN THE WORLD ... ENOUGH TO PLENTY FILL THE "LITTLE BOY" - THE CUTE NAME FOR THE ATOM BOMB DUMPED ON HIROSHIMA.

"That's no hint. Is it?" Cresty questions while tying the sleeves of the hooded sweatshirt around her waist, around me.

We walk through the Rutgers campus center

THE CHESS GAME

and cross over the cobblestones on narrow Penn Street, which isn't one way but can only squeeze one car by at a time. We head toward a grassy square block with a grand block of a building in the middle. We face the back of this... library. A really grand concrete structure with pillars.

"It looks like the Parthenon," Choker says.

"You don't need to show off your knowledge of ancient Greece," Cresty says. He replies, "Yes... I do. I need to... "

I'm pleased he does "show off" since I have learned so much from him... and Cresty, who talks to me when Choker isn't around. She knows I'm alive. I just find it odd that Cresty is going for this ultrasound, but she told Choker it was just a checkup with her girl specialist doc since her "plumbing is screwed up." No big deal. The photograph will show I'm alive.

There are no people around this impressive library, but there are a dozen or so benches for us to chose, for us to rest. All the chiseled concrete designed benches are under leafy trees with wide canopies. We sit.

On cue, a text from Ruby:

> IN THE EARLY 1900'S FOR ABOUT A QUARTER OF A CENTURY CAMDEN WAS

THE HEADQUARTES OF THE VICTOR TALKING MACHINE COMPANY... IT BECAME RCA AND MADE MOST OF THE WORLD'S PHONOGRAPHS... THEN GE BOUGHT THE CO. IN THE MID-1980'S... PROMISED TO KEEP THE BUILDING OPEN... SOON SOLD TO MARTIN MARIETTA... MERGED WITH LOCKHEED...

NOW L-3...

MY MOVE NF3

L-3 BUILDS COMMUNICATIONS AND INTELLIGENCE SYSTEMS FOR THE GOVERNMENT... DEPARTMENT OF DEFENSE... HOMELAND SECURITY... EVEN NASA ...

CLIFF'S MOVE QF6

"Didn't Ruby just move out of turn?" Cresty asks.

"Nope, remember, he opened with the French Defense," Choker says.

"Ya, your right."

A text from Cliff:

THE NEW BUILDING DIDN'T HELP THE CITY SCHOOLS... HAD TO BE TAKEN OVER BY

THE CHESS GAME

> THE STATE IN 2005... DIDN'T HELP THE PEOPLE... 40 PERCENT LIVED UNDER THE POVERTY LINE IN THE CITY... DIDN'T HELP THE CRIME... SIX TIMES HIGHER THAN THE NATIONAL AVERAGE... PERFECT PYRRHIC VICTORY...

Choker rests his head on Cresty's lap. He adjusts the sleeves of the hoodie to make a pillow. I can feel his breath. Another text from Ruby:

> BUT THEN WE GOT THE NEW POLICE DEPARTMENT... THEY WERE EVERYWHERE... LIKE A FLY ON THE WALL... CRIME IS DOWN AND SPIRITS UP

Choker flips the phone settings to his music and selects a song. He plays U2's "The Fly."

Cresty says, "Indeed, Bono pontificates how every artist is a cannibal, every poet is a thief" before Choker starts singing. He imitates Bono, mimicking his words with style and stress:

> *Our* baby child
> It's no secret that *people* are falling from the sky
> It's no secret that our world is in *madness with fright*

They say the sun is sometimes eclipsed *by noon*

He adjusts his belt, sits up and penetrates Cresty with his eyes, as if he knows about me. He continues:

> You know *no one sees* you when *you walk* in the room
> It's no secret that *the world* is *stuffed up, screaming for* help
> It's no secret that a *friar* won't *pray for one's self*
> *Hey*, say a secret *now* is something you tell *everyone else*
> So, I'm telling you *mild*
> *One* man will *sag*
> *One* man will *fall*
> On the *rear space to shove*
> Like a fly *in city hall*
> *This* no secret at all
> *This* no secret that a conscience can sometimes be a pest
> *This* no secret *population* bites the nails of success

Choker points to Cresty with both forefingers,

THE CHESS GAME

as if cueing her and then he sings:

> Every *creationist* is a cannibal, every *know-it* is a thief
> To kill their *creation* and *multiply* their grief
> *Masses shove*
> *O*ne man will rise
> *O*ne man will *sprawl*
> On the *rear space to shove*
> Like a fly *in city hall*
> *This* no secret at all
> *Eyes all* shine like a
> *exploding* star
> *All* falling from the sky
> *O*ne man will rise
> *O*ne man will s*prawl*
> On the *rear space to shove*
> Like a fly *in city hall*
> *This* no secret at all

Taking off his belt and tying it around his neck like a noose, Choker pulls and screams:

> *Bro,* yeah!
> It's no secret that *the masses* are falling from the sky
> The universe *imploded* 'cause of one man's lie

>Look, I gotta go, yeah I'm running outta *range*
>
>There's a lot of *people, who I cannot* rearrange

"You know," Cresty says to him, "Bono isn't actually singing about a fly. You know, right?"

"Huh?"

"A *man* will rise?" she says. "Who is the *only* man who rose?"

"LeBron King James?" Choker says playfully. "He left Cleveland and won a championship in Miami."

"Nope you dope. One man rose," Cresty says. "All men fall."

"How did ya know? I mean, how you figure that out?"

"I don't know. It's like a voice inside me. Like someone told me to think on a higher level.

"Or is telling me."

Looking down the street from the library, there is a church on the corner of Rutgers, across from the tennis courts. There are parking meters on the two streets flanking the church, but no cars are parked there. There is just a hearse parked in front of the 15-foot wooden red doors of the church.

A casket covered in a purple cloth and one

THE CHESS GAME

pallbearer wait for the doors to open to the Victory Temple Community Church as two students volley basketballs, using their hands as rackets across the street on the closest tennis court.

The homeless looking man wearing mirror sunglasses and an Abe Lincoln black stovepipe top hat slumps around the corner. He stops behind the casket and flashes the cardboard sign that reads: "The Wizard will fix everything."

THE CHESS GAME

Chapter 3

With the river at our backs, we sit on the concrete center staircase of Campbell's Field. A long home run over the leftfield wall would splash into the river. A shot to center would carom off the base of the Jersey-side support tower of the bridge. We are looking across Delaware Street to the Victor building with that red tower and the glass mosaic of Victor's talking dog, "Nipper," who stakes the best view of the stadium below.

The Camden Riversharks, a minor league baseball team, plays at Campbell's Field, across the river from where the Phillies play in the Major League. Really, the stadium edges up to the concrete tower foundation of the suspension bridge. The bridge is tucked into a recess where the river bends, as if an angel with silver wings dropped this modern facility from heaven onto this charred corner of the earth.

"Big bridge," Choker says for some reason.

"Ya. But not the Townsend's Inlet Bridge," Cresty says.

"Yup. But what bridge is?" Choker asks. "What bridge could be better than going from Sea Isle to Avalon… to play pickup basketball at dawn?"

"Not even the Garden State Parkway Bridge," Cresty says. "Not even as good as driving into

Cape May with the blind and mad Marion, our arborist employer... The Fish Finder at the wheel."

Cresty checks some information on her phone and tells Choker that for years, the State Prison sat opposite of the ballpark, on the other side of the Ben Franklin Bridge. She tells him, "however in the hopes of sparking economic growth in North Camden," the jail was demolished three years ago in 2010. She says how the acre of what should be prime riverfront real estate across from a major city still sits empty five years later with no concrete plans for development or any interest from developers.

She adds that the major growth area of Camden surrounds the college campus a few blocks up from the river and the bridge to Philly.

"You would think then, the king would be at a major university," Choker says.

"You mean the Wizard," Cresty says. "C'mon, bro. Think. You're the smart one here. The one who went to the prestigious private catholic high school in North Jersey... where all the money is because the cash ain't here in South Jersey's largest city."

"Smart one? Hell, my most memorable class ever in high school was a junior year sociology class when we listened to The Hotel California and

THE CHESS GAME

then talked about the meaning of the lyrics for 40 minutes," Choker says.

"Was it about drugs? You know, THC, The Hotel California or tetrahydrocannabinol, the active ingredient in marijuana," he continues like a college professor at the podium. "Did the Eagles play on initials like the Beatles' Lucy in the Sky with Diamonds… LSD… or were they singing about BF Skinner's teaching of the times on controlled behavior? You know, *'we are programmed to receive, you can check out any time you like but you can never leave.'* Or was it about behaving like Pavlov's Dogs? You know with *'we are all just prisoners here by our own device.'*

"Or was the song about the post '60s dark underbelly of America? You know, *'this could be heaven, or this could be hell.'*

"Maybe, it was just about simply a midwestern rock-n-roll band of boys dreaming of meeting a cool California girl? You know, *'the warm smell of colitas rising up through the air.'*"

"Colitas isn't even a word," Cresty injects.

"I thought, that's what we did," Choker says.

"How can you be so smart and so stupid at the same time?" she asks. "You know simultaneously smart and stupid…"

"I'm thinking it's the best lyrics, the most meaningful, to a song ever," Choker continues. "Maybe for all these meanings. And definitely for those 40 minutes making me think in high school and not memorize stuff... and still not know almost three years later.

"And it kept me for a few minutes of not dreaming of playing major college basketball and instead daydreaming of The Hotel California, *'with mirrors on the ceiling and pink champagne on ice'* on that lovely spring afternoon in high school ..."

"Man, you dug deep there. I think, my dad, and his Pete's Street Spiritualism is rubbing off on you," Cresty says, putting her arm around his strong shoulders, layered with muscles from all those years of doing fingertip pushups. "Bro, you're dropping names like B.F. *foo-kin* Skinner ... better watch it or the B.F. Bridge here will faint and fall on us... we should have a morning mimosa with this erudite talk."

"Says here," Choker adds, looking at his phone, "that the Ben Franklin Bridge was the longest suspension bridge in the world when built in 1926. Maybe the king is on top of one of the towers... it would have to be the Jersey-side one above the field... right? To be in Camden, right?"

"You mean the Wizard," is all Cresty answers.

THE CHESS GAME

An older man carrying a painter's bucket and a fishing rod strolls toward us along with another older man in a motorized wheelchair with a fishing rod stretched across his lap. Mornie?

No, it's not him, the man under the frozen clock.

The painter bucket man and the wheelchair man don't hesitate to approach us. They look to be about the same age of Cliff and Ruby. They stop.

"Mighty, mighty number seven," the man with the bucket says, pointing to Choker's jersey. "You know, seven is the number of perfection and completeness in the Bible."

"And," the man in the wheelchair adds, "on the seventh day, God rested."

"I knew that," Choker says almost defiantly.

"Hey, did you know, Bob Dylan played here almost 10 years ago now?" the man with the bucket says pointing to the stadium. "All 7,007 seats were sold."

"Just like it was filled for the ceremony when it opened in 1999 and then governor Christine Todd Whitman christened the park that was built from public and private monies… and of course Rutgers University," the man in the wheel chair recites. "Now, now it's empty.

"Empty as the man's shopping cart," the bucket man says. He nods toward the homeless-looking man in the L. L. Bean vest wearing mirror sunglasses and the Abe Lincoln black stovepipe top hat who is a block down Delaware Avenue. The man is standing inside the gate below the Ben Franklin Bridge, where maintenance trucks are parked with workers inside eating breakfast sandwiches from 7-11.

The man with the bucket taps Choker on the head and points across the river, away from the man with the shopping cart. Choker turns to look back at the Abe Lincoln hat man, but he is tapped on the head again and nudged to look toward Philadelphia.

"You know it was the Quakers who crossed the river and settled in Camden back in 1687 or so. You can see William Penn standing on top of City Hall across the river looking back at us sitting here on Delaware and Penn streets."

"Hope he points and finds the fish for you," Choker says. "He was known to be a Fish Finder."

"There was a gentleman's agreement that no building would be taller than Penn's flattop and wide-brimmed hat, but Liberty Place was built in 1985, putting Penn in its shadow," the bucket man says, nodding over to the green glass structure with

THE CHESS GAME

the magnificent pointed steeple towering over the statue of the Quaker giant."

Choker looks back again to the gated section under the bridge. The homeless looking man in the L. L. Bean vest is gone.

"Man, the man with the shopping cart packs some mysterious ways behind those mirror sunglasses," Choker says, certainly prodding for the two men to tell him who he is, "and under the Abe Lincoln black stovepipe top hat."

"*Ways* is all we have," the wheelchair man says, gently rolling forward to us and then quickly backing up. "Mysterious or glorious or shirtless, *ways* is all we have."

"Or had. Like the stadium. Named after Campbell Soup. The company bought the naming right," the other man rattles, now sitting on his bucket. "The Camden Riversharks started playing here in 2001. They play in the Independent Atlantic League."

"Didn't play as well as Bob Dylan," the man says spinning his wheelchair in a circle. "The Riversharks left town and the stadium is empty now.

"Well, of course, the Rutgers baseball team plays here."

"And KYW-TV still broadcasts from there with

a weather camera," the bucket man says.

"The field couldn't stick around as long as its much older namesake," the wheelchair man huffs. "Campbell Soup was started by two men from South Jersey. One man, Joseph Campbell a merchant from Bridgeton, and another, Abraham Anderson, who built iceboxes, back in 1867 or so.

"Campbell Soup is now slurped in 120 countries."

"And back in the 60's Andy Warhol took the Campbell soup can and made it into silkscreens," the bucket man says. "His pop art was duplicates of the cans but then became more funky, like his celebrity silkscreens. Silky, huh?"

"How do you gentlemen know all this?" Cresty asks politely.

"We live here," they both say at once.

"The city is our home," the bucket man says.

"Its history is our history," the wheelchair man adds.

Choker's cell buzzes. It is Cliff. He texts the moves: d4 Bd6. Choker tries to explain, but the two fishermen walk and wheel away. Cliff sends another text:

> MY DAD WAS PLAYING CHESS BY HIMSELF ON THE RAFT WHEN ANGEL FLOPPED ON

THE CHESS GAME

THE ONE-MAN RAFT... DEMANDED TO PLAY... MY DAD OPENED WITH THE KING PAWN FORWARD TWO SPACES TO E4... ATLANTIC CITY MAN FOLLOWED WITH HIS BISHOP PAWN TWO SPACES TO F5... THE MAN WITH SLICKED HAIR LAUGHED AT MY DAD ...

We wander past the brick stadium with the green roof and steps rising up the middle. We sit briefly in the picnic area outside left-field foul pole. We lounge in the grass between the parking lot and the Riverwalk before actually walking to the river. There are rocks the size of bases in baseball on the embankment of the river. We sit on the large, flat rocks.

Choker plays his music, looking over the river and away from us, he sings his words for U2's With or Without You:

> See *reality* set in your eyes
> See the *unborn* twist *inside*
> I wait for *two*
> Sleight of hand and *without hate*
> On a *train without rails baby won't* wait
> *The world waits*, without you
> With or without *two*

With or without *two*
Through the *born* we reach the shore
You give it all but *can't have* more
And I'm waiting for *two*
With or without *two*
With or without *two*
World can't live
With or without *two*

"You know bro, the song isn't about… a girl, the real words I mean," Cresty says.

I want to tell them Bono is singing about Jesus. Just as I think this, Cresty says, "The song isn't about a girl, or a guy, a lover. Don't you get the giveaway line? The clue is right there in 'the thorn twist in your side?' "

Choker just keeps singing:

And *we* give *ourselves* away
And *we* give
And *we* give
And *we* give *ourselves* away
The farms are tied
Food supply bruised, *world's left* me with
Nothing *but sin* and
Nothing left *but dues*
And *we* give *ourselves* away

THE CHESS GAME

And *we* give *ourselves* away
And *we* give
And *we* give
And *we* give *ourselves* away
With or without *two*
With or without *two*
World can't live
With or without *two*
Oh
With or without *two*
With or without *two*

Choker turns to Cresty, holds her like he is dancing and then dips her backwards as he belts:

We can't live
With or without *a few*
With or without *a few*

I hope they feel the same way about me. Or will I be the boy in the black and white grainy photograph that will never be?

We wander by the benches under a pavilion built with concrete and steel facing the river.

"The quay," Cresty says.

City folks are feeding birds on the quay… I guess, learning a new word. Two birds fight for the same scrap. "Like the basketball courts in Avalon," Choker says about the birds, "but without the mommies in tight tennis outfits."

Looking south, down river, we can see the battleship, the New Jersey. The Camden towers of the Victor, with Nipper the dog, and City Hall are to our left. The red hands of the clock on the City Hall tower say its 9:06... but is an hour behind.

A young guy carrying books under one arm while riding a bike asks if we can spare 70 cents.

"Don't matter if you are a poet or a punk," Choker sings as the guy pedals by, not even slowing down for an answer, "don't have 70 cents to bare, let alone spare."

We turn away, looking toward our right, to the west, to see Penn's hat on top of the statue above City Hall in Philadelphia and with Liberty Place serving as a backdrop. And off in the distance we see the steel rising above the magnificent glass structure of a business building.

Tucked in the corner where the white railing of the redbrick walkway turns, sits the one man on the bucket and the other man in the wheelchair. Only the man on the bucket is fishing. The rod remains stretched across the lap of the man in the wheelchair.

"We will catch something today," the

wheelchair man says, tapping his friend's head.

"Yeah today is the day," the man on the bucket says. "We'll catch something we can eat, feed others, too... not hook another old Campbell soup can."

"Keep the faith," Cresty says. "Keep up your *ways*."

"*Ways*," the man in the wheelchair says, "is our faith."

Wandering south toward the battleship, with a tug boat churning toward the bridge to our right, Cresty says, "You know, bro, that's what Bono is singing about in 'With or Without You.'"

"You don't say. Do you?" Choker says while looking back at the two men fishing, but I think he is really checking for the homeless looking man in the L.L Bean vest wearing mirror sunglasses and the Abe Lincoln black stovepipe top hat with the empty shopping cart.

"I do say. Or Bono does say, how it's so *fooking* hard to live with faith in God... but how you can't get through this world without faith in Him."

"Well," Choker says, rubbing her head, "You know, as the man says, you must have your *ways*."

"*Ways*," Cresty says, rubbing me, "is all we have."

THE CHESS GAME

Chapter 4

We are moving across the city, wandering south along the Delaware River with our eyes peeled open for the man pushing the shopping cart. The burning smell of the tugboat engine pushing a cargo ship up river chokes us. Choker and Cresty stop to stare at a stray dog sniffing the fumes. The mixed black and dark brown German Shepherd stands alone on the Riverwalk, looking back at us, sniffing. The dog's oddly shaped left ear droops.

Ahead, and above, the white globe-shaped dome of the aquarium adds a bit of variety, some shape and intrigue, to the square buildings and structures along the "seascape," as Cresty calls the view on both sides of the river. Or, as Choker told her, "The dome makes the roof look like half of a golf ball."

He makes an air golf swing at the ball, yelling "fore" and startling the snorting dog.

"I wonder if my *sea* men can swim like the fishes in the aquarium?" Choker taunts. He feigns another golf swing as if to drive the lonely dog across the river and onto the skating rink at Penn's Landing. "Guess we'll never know with you... with your plumbing. Huh?"

Cresty is focused on a lady, perhaps in her

fifties, dressed in a black mink coat with a matching furry black pillbox hat. The lady is walking with erratic steps toward us. She peeks into her purse, abruptly turns around, and walks away saying only, "Oops."

Choker switches from his mock golf swing to playfully dribbling an invisible basketball and pulling up to take jump shots into the river when his phone rings, or chimes. Cresty studies the confused woman as she bounces away with her hand over her fancy hat.

"Hey Ruby Tuesday," Choker answers, clicking on the speaker.

"Hey, you still hanging onto the Rolling Stones' references?" the voice says.

"Oh," Choker says. "Sorry, I didn't look at who was calling. I thought it was this guy we met named Ruby. Hey dad."

"Just calling to say 'hey.' You ok?"

"Up in Camden with Cresty. She has a doc appointment."

"She ok?"

"Yup," Choker says. "I mean, oh yeah."

"Camden? I just got a text from one of my former high school teammates who asked if Clarence Turner, the former Camden High basketball coach, just died? We played against his

THE CHESS GAME

powerhouse team in 1979 with the smooth Billy Culbertson and the iceman Milt Wagner."

"Was Billy Thompson and Kevin Walls on that team?" Choker asks.

"Thank God no," the voice in the phone says. "No, they were too young."

"I will ask around town if Coach Turner died. Got to go, the doc wants to see us," Choker says, clicking off the phone. The phone chimes immediately. The church bells ring only twice before Choker answers.

"Hey Busta, playing the Game of Chess are you? Now I just wanted to let you know to check out the Adventure Aquarium," Ruby informs us. "That be if finding adventure in a building is your thingy."

"A hint?" Choker asks. "*Is* that a hint? Huh? Ruby Tuesday?"

"Opened in 1992 as the New Jersey State Aquarium, but the dang state pulled out too," Ruby continues without acknowledging Choker's question. "Suppos'd to be the king piece to revitalize the castle of Camden."

"Air ball on that one, huh," Choker says. He pumps his fist for no reason.

Cresty looks at her phone. She scrolls a bit.

"Ahhh, here it is…I hear, inside the Aquarium,

there is a Jules Verne Gallery," Cresty says.

"All pieces of the Cacophony of Camden," Cliff says into the speakerphone, "Blooming right, you are journeying to the center of the earth like Jules did."

"The sharks busta," Ruby says. "There'd be sharks all over the center of the aquarium... but no clues where the Wizard is."

"There were sharks, mister Ruby, all over the crew of the USS Indy," Cliff says softly.

"Did yer know there are two sharks inside all of us?" Ruby blurts out. "Right there with the Wizard and with Jesus. Yer know one shark is angry and evil. The other shark is loving and joyful."

"The story goes," Cliff interrupts, "that one of the sailors from the USS Indy told this story to another scared sailor while floating in the South Pacific. Now Ruby tells it like the story is his parable.

"Ruby knows what the sailor said," Ruby continues, "The sailor said that the two sharks would fight each other inside of him. It would be a battle to the death between the two sharks until we are rescued... by Jesus.

"The scared sailor asked the storytelling sailor as their mates were being eaten, which shark would win?" Cliff injects. "He replied, 'the shark you

THE CHESS GAME

feed.'"

A worker dressed in a shark costume pulls out of the aquarium parking lot in a dented car and asks us for directions. Choker points to City Hall.

"The coke bottle building is in the center of the city, that's all we really know," he says.

The costume person asks, "What time is it? Must be feeding time."

Choker points to the clock on top of City Hall.

"It is an hour behind," Cresty tells the costumed worker and looks at her phone before adding, "there's an exhibit inside called Shark Realm. Right?"

The worker dressed in the shark costume says, "That's my realm" and then speeds out of the aquarium parking lot, turning and revealing both sides of the car is dented.

"Like a king's realm... "Cliff starts to say on Choker's speakerphone before being interrupted by Ruby, who says, "You mean like a Wizard," and then Cliff finishes by saying, "Right... who rules his realm like the sharks rule the ocean."

"And like Rube rules the Game of Chess," Ruby says. "Like the Wizard rules the streets of Camden. Like the man behind the curtains in the tower rules the city."

"Only, mister Ruby, if the Wizard," Cliff says,

"will be the ostensible Wizard who will serve."

"The Wizard has... has to find his *ways*, too," Ruby says definitively, "like the rest of *youse*."

"You speak with dogmatic confidence as if the Wizard isn't your chimera," Cliff says with the matter-of-factness of a college professor. "There is a dissonance... '

"This dissonance is good," Ruby interrupts as if his intellect is suddenly stimulated. "If yer believe something is indeed *specious*, well, Master Cliff, it is good you say.

"After all, you are the one who studies *phrenology* along with your mandarin."

"Hah, you're the one who studies more than me," Cliff says. "You read Walt Whitman. You study his philosophies like you're on your own death bed."

"Only because," Ruby says stopping suddenly. He then recites:

> *There was never any more inception than there is now,*
> *Nor any more youth or age than there is now,*
> *And will never be any more perfection than there is now,*
> *Nor any more heaven or hell than there is*

THE CHESS GAME

now.

"In Songs of Myself, WW teaches us," Ruby says, "he teaches us that the 'I' is all powerful."

We continue our meandering walk along the river toward the aquarium, stopping next to the building with the golf ball roof in front of an open field filled with blooming red flowers.

"Did you hear him?" Choker asks Cresty. "He said 'the king piece to revitalize the castle of Camden' was the aquarium."

Cresty nods, but not convincingly like she believes.

"You would think the king would be at the aquarium." Choker reasons.

"You mean the Wizard," Cresty says. "But he said the chess piece wasn't inside. You didn't hear him."

We look all around the outside of the aquarium, circling the gardens and the turnstiles twice, before we turn around and walk back toward the blue bridge of rusting steel with the tugboat still churning smog underneath. The fishermen are gone. The bucket is there, and the wheelchair is there, but the two men are gone.

Ruby calls again:

"You know the Wizard had to replace the three

Camden mayors locked up for corruption...

"Angelo Errichetti took a bribe from FBI undercover agents for helping a fake Arab sheikh immigrate into the country back in 1981.

"In '99, Arnold Webster, the former superintendent of Camden schools, paid himself from school district funds after he became mayor.

"Then Milton Milan took payoffs from the Philly mob, free renovations on his house from Camden vendors and even laundered the Wizard's money."

We look up and see the red hands of the Roman numeral clock on City Hall. The clock says its 10:10 ... but is an hour behind.

Cliff sends a text:

> AFTER MY DAD OPENED WITH THE KING PAWN FORWARD TWO SPACES TO E4 AND THE ATLANTIC CITY MAN FOLLOWED WITH HIS BISHOP PAWN TWO SPACES TO F5 MY DAD ATTACKED WITH HIS ADVANCED PAWN ON THE DIAGONAL E4XF5 TO CAPTURE THE MAN WITH SLICKED HAIR ADVANCE PAWN ... ANGEL TOOK THE BAIT AND MOVED HIS KNIGHT PAWN FORWARD TWO SPACES TO G5 ...

THE CHESS GAME

Turning north again, we make a left down a redbrick sidewalk with a grass median strip and toward the Nipper Tower of the Victor.

A college-looking girl and a guy, who looks younger than she are holding hands. He is carrying a stack of books. They are dressed in colorful and light clothing as if they know how happy and hot they will be today.

Choker starts singing along with U2's ballad "One" that is playing on his phone:

> Is *justice* getting better
> Or do you feel the *blame*
> Will it make *life hungrier for* you
> Now *another* someone to *shame*
> You say
> *Shun* love
> *Shun* life
> When *no* one feed

The cute couple both stare with fixed stone-faced smiles. Cresty claps and smiles at them, trying to gain their attention. She thinks they just look *too* happy compared to us. I wonder… are Choker and Cresty happy? Or are they faking whatever happiness is?

Choker continues faking being Bono:

In the night
It's one *stove*
We get to share it
It leaves you baby
If you don't *look* for it
Did I disappoint you?
Or leave *without* taste in your mouth?
You act like you never had love
And you want me to go without
Well it's too late
Tonight
To drag the past out
Into the light
We're one
But we're not *to blame*
We get to *bury* each other
Bury each other
Shun

 Cresty nods approvingly to the cute couple, whose odd smiles stay frozen.
 "You know, bro, the song isn't about boy-girl love," she says.
 "Of course it is," Choker says. "Don't tell me it is about girl-girl love."

THE CHESS GAME

"No Bono sings about the challenge of finding Jesus amongst your peers, how joining together with your closest of friends to try and believe is hard, and so is trying to find God on your own," she rattles. "Sing the words."

Choker sings, making up his own words again with emphasis:

> Have *we* come here for forgiveness
> Have *we* come to raise the dead
> Have *we* come here to play Jesus
> To the lepers in *our* head
> Did *we* ask too much
> More than a lot
> You gave me nothing
> Now it's all *we* got
> We're one
> But we're not the same
> We hurt each other
> Then we do it again
> You say
> Love *isn't simple*
> Love *the tower* law

Choker stops, listens and then says *Jesus...* and sings:

Love is a temple
Love the higher law
Jes... ask me to enter
But then you made me crawl
And I can't be holding on
To what you got
When all *Jes*... got is hurt
One love
One blood
One life
You got to do what you should
One life
With each other
Sisters
Brothers
One life
But we're not the same
We get to carry each other
Carry each other
One
One

  The white and blue River LINE crosses in front of the Victor. We stop and wait.
  Turning around, we see the towers of Philadelphia behind the aquarium business building, The Mickle building stands to the left. In

THE CHESS GAME

front of the Mickle, the TEDDY HINSON waterfront garage looks like a concrete fort protecting the river and the Susquehanna Bank music center to the left. Behind the sprawling concert amphitheater lawn is the USS New Jersey.

Cliff calls: "Bc4 Nc6." He adds, "If you wander to the Fairview Section of Camden, stop at 3072 S. Constitution Ave., where I still live with the pumice chess set my dad clutched when the Navy picked him up. He brought it back to the Fairview, but not his best friend from Congress Avenue behind us. He stayed within the sharks."

The lady, the one in her fifties, dressed in a fake black mink coat with a matching furry black pillbox hat is walking straight toward us. Her steps aren't erratic anymore. She is holding the leash of the German Shepherd.

"Excuse me," she says, "Pardon me. Did you see a homeless looking man in a L. L. Bean vest and mirror sunglasses pushing the empty shopping cart?"

"We did."

"Where?"

"Back there," Choker says pointing toward the bridge. "He is wearing an Abe Lincoln black stovepipe top hat."

"I know, he says its Abe's lid," she says as if

she believes and then looks quickly into her purse.

"The Abe Lincoln?" Choker asks incredulously.

"No way," Cresty bristles.

"Way," she says and walks briskly away with the dog following, "he says he is related to Boston Corbett, the man who shot the man who shot Lincoln ... that's all I know, bro."

"Hey," Choker says, "Did you see the fishermen? The guy with the bucket and the guy in the wheelchair?"

"Oh, they probably swam out again in the river," she says without turning around. "They probably are helping to push the tiny tugboat."

We run to the river. Cresty is ahead of Choker. We pick up the pace when we see the empty wheelchair and upside-down bucket. As we reach the white railing, we see the two fishermen sitting, with shoes off and feet stretch out into the river.

"Hey, you ok? Cresty asks.

Without turning around, they say together "never better."

"Well, whatcha doin?" she asks in somewhat relief.

"Our dogs need to find their ways, too," they say together. "Whatcha you two be doin?"

"We were worried," Cresty begins to say before Choker injects, "We heard Clarence Turner died.

THE CHESS GAME

Did you know him?"

"Know him! Went to all the games at The High. Everyone in the city did," the bucket man says. "He was the king on the Castle on the Hill over by the river on Baird Boulevard."

"The king?" Choker asks.

"Yeah, the coach," the bucket man says.

"I would leave work early since The High only played afternoon games," the wheelchair man says. "I would yell at the uncolored folk who came in the gym to 'sit in the back of the gym.'"

The bucket man taps his bucket with a short drum roll.

"I was a janitor at the school," the bucket man continues. "I used to hear all his pregame speeches. He would end each speech before the game the same."

Another drum roll on the bucket.

"The team would put their hands in the huddle and then lift them up as Coach Turner would say, 'Johnny Luckett' and the boys would respond with the rhyme 'mother… '

"Don't want to cuss in front of you youngins."

"Yeah he could coach," the wheelchair man says. "His teams won 775 games, 22 South Jersey titles and seven state titles. His 1986 squad was picked number one in the nation after the season by

USA Today.

"And Coach Clarence played minor league baseball with t*he* Jackie Robinson."

"Did he die? No," the bucket man says. "We would've heard."

"We heard that hoax before," the wheelchair man says getting up and walking over the rocks, climbing the railing and sitting in the wheelchair to put on his shoes. "We heard that hoax before."

Cresty hops the rail and negotiates the rocks all the way to the water line. She reaches between the rocks and grabs a handful of sand. She tosses the sand toward the river. Half blows back and sticks to her old number 24 jersey.

"I need the Magnetic Reversion Reversal therapy," she says. "This city needs MRR."

The bucket man taps his bucket slowly and then speeds into a drum roll. He is cueing Cresty to explain. She does.

"Pete taught us how Magnetic Reversion is simply the things that initially bring people together ultimately drive them apart... for example, the city of Camden brought all these people together, but now the failing city is driving people away."

The bucket man taps his bucket to the slow beat of a ticking clock.

THE CHESS GAME

"Praying to Pete," she says nodding her head to the beat, "that the MRR works for me... and this city."

THE CHESS GAME

Chapter 5

Without any urgency, we wander up Market Street, with every curious step under the watchful tilted eye of Nipper up lofted in the Victor. The stained-glass window of the iconic dog and the historic phonograph leads us away from the river and on toward the lure of the City Hall clock tower.

On the next block stands an abandoned brick factory that looks as if it was once an original RCA building, too, like the Victor. But this obtrusive eyesore of a structure has been long forgotten.

A second growth of trees pokes through the broken windows of the first two floors of the empty eight-story building near the end of Market. Up another block, the majestic National State Bank also sits empty on the corner of Second and Market. The two-story structure that looks like it was built with the same concrete as City Hall and appears like it could open at noon with a few tellers if money suddenly flowed its way.

With no plan of where to go, we wander up the tree-lined street and past the abandoned bank. Two homeless men are sitting on the concrete bench in front of the bank and two women slump on another bench around the corner.

One of the men crosses the street with us and plucks a white plastic trash bag from a black metal trashcan in front of Hank's Restaurant. The trash bag is tied at the top. He digs inside the bag looking certain of finding hidden loot. It looks as if he is withdrawing cash from a savings account in the empty bank he guards. The man walks back across the street to the bank. On the back of his black hoodie reads "Hank's Restaurant" in faded white letters.

A cheerful parking lot security guard waves at us from across Market Street. The guard, who is sitting in a red booth with a green roof no bigger than a closet, flaps his hand out the sliding door. Cars fill the federal jury parking lot he watches on the corner of Third and Market.

We cross the street, crossing on the diagonal, jaywalking like all the Camdeners seem to do, as if it is a sport to dodge disinterested traffic. We wave to the guard as we step onto the red bricks with odd yellow gas markings "G12" on this side of Market Street.

"I'm waving to almost everyone," he says. "It's my 40th anniversary on the job. My first day was the opening morning of the trial for the Camden 28 back in the summer of 1973."

"Congrats, sir, but that would make this your 42nd anniversary," Choker says, looking down at the "G12" markings and then looking up in time to

THE CHESS GAME

see the man across the street put the white bag back into the black trash can. With amused eyes, Cresty pulls his arm and we edge closer to the booth.

"The Camden 28?" she says with an innocent but interrogatory tone. "Were they criminals?"

"Yeah. Were they bank robbers?" Choker asks. "A gang? Like Bonnie and Clyde? Or, perhaps, maybe the John Dillinger gang?

"I read, though, that bank robberies are down almost 70 percent these days from its heyday over a quarter of a century ago. I read the average haul now is just under $7,000. Not even enough to pay for one class in a semester at Ursinus College."

"What? Are you two looking to knock off a bank in the city?" the guard, a jowly-cheeked man with a stiff white collared shirt, asks while straightening his solid blue tie. "I don't even think there is any money in any of the banks in town anymore. Save yourself the trouble. Plus, the new police force is good. You will be nabbed before you reach Walt Whitman's grave on the outskirt of South Camden.

"And no, the Camden 28 weren't bank robbers. The group of Catholics and other religious types were harmless anti-Vietnam War protestors. They raided the draft board on the fourth floor of the post office and the courthouse over there," he said grinning and pointing to the four-story concrete building across the street. An eagle is engraved on the wall on either side of the front steps.

"The great Fr. Michael Doyle was their leader. He is still the pastor at my parish in South Camden, Sacred Heart. He is a gift from God."

"Doesn't look like God left many gifts here," Cresty says.

The man does some slanted pushups against the desktop in his booth before he continues talking.

"Monsignor Doyle now, and the Camden 28 were the rage around the country 40 years ago," he says, straightening his solid blue tie again. "In 1973, I was just home a few days, a few pot-smoking days after serving two years in Vietnam, and landed this job."

"But that would be 42…" Choker begins to say when the guard adds, "I've seen it all… the fall. I know everyone… the ones who were jailed mostly."

"Did you hear if Clarence Turner died?" Choker asks.

The guard man must not have heard the question since he answered the others. With his tie flipped over his left shoulder, he leans up against his desk with both hands and resumes doing his angled pushups.

THE CHESS GAME

We continue strolling up Market, heading east into the elevated sun. We jaywalk across the street in front of an empty lot that is sandwiched between two row homes that are separated by four thick metal bars holding up each side of the bare brick walls. We wander past a blue dumpster stuffed with crushed cinder blocks that is blocking a lane in the street in front of a dilapidated building. We head toward the United States Post Office and Courthouse, which is surrounded by a half-dozen concrete flowerpots blocking one lane of the road.

A bit out of breath, the jovial security guard scoots behind us and up the front steps. He taps the engraved eagle where we sit down on the landing of the three steps.

"Break time, the lot if full anyway," he says, pointing to the City Hall clock that says its 10:30… but is an hour behind.

"Want a soda? I once bought Supreme Court Justice William Brennan a soda, actually a pop back then, inside here during the Camden 28 trial. He later called it 'one of the greatest.'"

"One of the greatest soda pops?" Choker asks.

"One of the great trials of the 20th Century,'' he says. "The Justice didn't offer an opinion on the soda pop.

"Are you here to do a documentary on the

Camden 28? If so, it's been done. But the documentary didn't mention Judge Brennan was even more famous since he was a Roman Catholic and he was also the justice that legalized abortion earlier that same year, my first as a guard here, in January of 1973."

"Yup, Ro-something vs. *ways*," Choker says.

"It was odd, though, he remained a strict foe of the death penalty, but he supported abortion," the guard says. "And he was one of eight children who grew up in Newark in North Jersey.

"His mother was a McDermott. I always wondered if she was related to the good Monsignor McDermott in East Camden, who is the pastor of St. Joe Pro."

The young guy carrying books under one arm while riding his bike reaches out his hand. The guard slaps in some change as the biker asks us "if we can spare 70 cents" again.

"He wasn't much older than me when I took the guard job, or your biker friend there when Monsignor McDermott left a -evel job in the Bishop's Office to come back and serve the people of his home parish," the guard says. "I think of him as a modern-day saint. Just like I do Monsignor Doyle. And Monsignor Michael Mannion, who is the pastor of the Cathedral here downtown.

THE CHESS GAME

"These three Irish Catholic priests have stabilized their sections of Camden above the rising flood waters of crime and corruption. The three saviors from Ireland were just the opposite of The Three Mayors of Camden who were elected by their own neighbors and then took their people's trust to jail.

"Those three church steeples where The Three Monsignors serve might not rise as high as City Hall, but they tower above it. McDermott, Mannion and Doyle are as immovable as the concrete flower pots here."

The guard does a dozen more slanted pushups against the end flower pot with an empty handle bottle of vodka standing upright and its burnt cap used to cook heroin under a budding flower.

"Good for the city that the Camden 28 jurors didn't send Monsignor Doyle to prison… sure you don't want a soda? Don't drink the Camden *wooder*."

The biker rides back again and the guard slaps more change into his outstretched hand. He uses the other hand to hold onto the handlebars while squeezing the books under his arm. "I read a lot in that booth of mine. Stop by if you want any Camden history. I know it all, as I said, seen it all over the last 40 years that I stopped counting the years… just watching the fall. But no one cares. You are the only ones who listen. Well Justice Brennan listened when I bought him that pop."

"Brennan, huh?" Cresty asks.

"That's the name of our friend's dog," Choker adds. "Our crazy Cape May friend Marion, The Fish Finder, who would be interested in talking with you…"

"Yeah, he was the seventh longest serving Supreme Court justice," the security guard says, pointing to Choker's Number seven jersey.

"Did you know in the Old Testament, there are just seven men who are named as a Man of God?" the guard questions. "Like I might have mentioned, but I'm not boasting, I do a lot of reading in that phone box of a booth."

"And pushups," Choker says.

"Who are they?" Cresty asks as Choker says, "Two are Moses and David."

"Everyone knows them," Cresty adds.

"Does everyone know Igdaliah? Elisha and Elijah? And… Samuel and Shemaiah?" the guard asks, his smile widening.

"How would anyone know their names?" Choker asks.

"Why wouldn't you know someone known as a Man of God?" the guard questions quickly with his

THE CHESS GAME

cheeks flapping, like in anger. "You should, at least, get to know The Three Monsignors.

"Get to know the Camdener's Three Men of God... McDermott, Mannion and Doyle."

"Do you know, did you hear if Clarence Turner died?" Choker asks again.

The guard man doesn't seem to hear him again as he watches Cresty do toe raises on the stairs of the courthouse while the guy on the bike turns around again in the middle of Market Street and flips a burnt bottle cap into the end flower pot.

We wander past a two-story law office building on the corner of Fourth and Market. There is pack of birds, one with a white-eye ring, munching on a pile of seed on the sidewalk. An office lady with straightened black hair laying neatly on her shoulders and wearing a wrinkled dark skirt below her knees opens the door to A. S. Woodruff Law and adds to the mound of bird seed from her blazer pocket.

"Nice," Cresty says.

"Yes," she says. "The building was added to the National Register of Historic Places.

"The birds," Cresty says.

"Oh, the Hermit thrush has a song that is the finest in nature, flute like beginning than several descending notes, related by harmonic simple integer pitch rates like most human music... I like to hear them sing under my office window."

A white double-cab pickup truck slows down. Three white-jumpsuit dressed men stare at us. With its front brakes grinding, the white double-cab pickup truck stops. The man in the back hands the office lady a new bag of birdseed.

The men in the truck continue to stare at us. Choker reties his thick-soled hiking boots on a metal spit rail fence. No, they aren't staring at us. They wait for the River LINE to chug by. The driver bobs his head to the sound of the train... click-clack-click-clack-click-clack ...

"I think I want to play basketball again. Think Ruby will really give me his red sneakers if we find the chess piece, the king?" Choker asks.

"You mean the Wizard," Cresty says.

We wander and continue up a few blocks, past City Hall, to the corner where a brown fieldstone church is surrounded by a black metal fence with pointed tips like arrows. The point of the steeple is as sharp as the fence tips and the brown spiral of the cathedral is topped off with a gold cross. The shining cross on top reflects the sun on a homeless person curled on the steps below.

"Monsignor Mannion?" Choker asks.

"No. I'm not him," the homeless person curled

on the steps says.

"Yes, no, I'm asking if he is in?" Choker says.

"This is the Cathedral of the Immaculate Conception, a Catholic church, a monsignor would be here," the man says, curling tighter on the steps. "The cornerstone out front says it was built in 1864."

Choker says, "Built in the middle of the Civil War."

Cresty scrolls on her phone. The man, looking up to show he wears an eye patch, says, "Don't need to read your phone, honey, in 2003 the Cathedral was listed on the National Register of Historic Places."

Inside, kneeling in pews beyond rows of lit candles, churchgoers recite the Fourth Luminous Mystery before the noon mass.

Choker says he never heard of this rosary while attending "holy St. Anthony's High" in North Jersey. So Cresty explains to him how "the great Pope John Paul II instituted these acts of service by Jesus." She kneels and says a quick prayer; I know how to pray, too.

Standing, Choker Googles the Fourth Luminous Mystery: The Transfiguration

In the back corner of the church leans a wooden shelf with books and pamphlets. Cresty pulls out a paperback on the Romero Center Ministries. The shelf creaks. "The Romero retreat building is located in the old covenant of the St. Joseph Pro-Cathedral, the Catholic parish in East Camden," she says.

Cresty reads how the Romero Center was dedicated properly on March 24, 1998 under pastor Monsignor Robert McDermott, "a former altar boy who came back to shepherd his neighborhood as a priest," just like the parking lot guard said. The ceremony was on the 18th anniversary of the assassination of Archbishop Oscar Romero of El Salvador.

"Says here Romero fought against poverty and social injustice," Cresty says, flipping to the back cover of the pamphlet. "He was shot offering mass in the chapel of a hospital called the Divine Providence."

"Some providence," Choker says. "Doesn't seem divine."

"Pope Francis started his beatification," Cresty continues, "praising him as a 'hero of liberation theology.'"

"He was a member of Opus Dei," the man with the eye patch says while poking his head inside the church doors.

"We had a friend in Sea Isle named Dei,"

THE CHESS GAME

Choker tells the man, who already has pulled his head back out the door.

Cresty shoves the pamphlet inside her number 24 jersey and tucks the paperback inside the elastic of her cutoff sweatpants. Choker holds the door open for her.

"You should visit the other Catholic cathedral in town, St. Joe Pro, indeed Camden has been forgotten so bad that it needs two cathedrals," the man with the eye patch says, curling back on the outside steps says. "There was another St. Joe's, but that was St. Joseph Polish Catholic Church in old Pollock Town in South Camden. I played in the last basketball game there in 1979. An Irish guy wearing an elbow pad from Camden Catholic hit a half court shot, well right across the half court line, on a Sunday morning to beat us. And Fr. McDermott was the coach, before he became a monsignor... and when he wore a thick mustache.

"Now old St. Joe Pro... it's now an old age home."

We head west, wandering back down Market Street toward the river with Philadelphia looming in the background. The River LINE clanks by us as small birds munch on the seed pile outside the lawyer's office.

The contented birds chirp and the train clickclacks in the background as Choker mimics U2's Yahweh:

> *See* these *Hoe's*
> Click-clacking *while* some dead *beat tweets*
> Take *her* shoes
> And *don't mean sheet*
> Take *her skirt*
> Polyester white trash *matted with hair*
> Take *her skirt*
> And make *a dream, dream*
> Take *her* soul
> *Branded* in some skin and bones
> Take *her* soul
> And make it *bling, bling*
> *Yah Yeah*, Yahweh

We sit on the end flower planter at the Post Office. Cresty rubs her belly. The massage soothes and feels lovely. We can see the shinning cross on top of the Cathedral's steeple surrounded by scaffolding.

Choker sings more of his Yahweh:

> Always pain before a child is born
> *Yah Yeah*, Yahweh
> Still, I'm *longing* for the dawn

THE CHESS GAME

> Take *babe's* hands
> *Give* them *chance* to carry
> Take *babe's* hands
> Don't make a fist, no
> Take *babe's* mouth
> So quick to *circumcise*
> Take *babe's* mouth
> Give *lips* a kiss
> *Yah Yeah*, Yahweh
> Always pain before the child is born

Cresty rubs her belly again. The touch, the feel… really feels good. Choker stands on the flower planter, glances over to the golden Cathedral's steeple smothered by scaffolding, back at the engravings of the eagle near us, and flaps his arms and sings:

> *Yah Yeah*, Yahweh
> Still, I'm *longing* for the dawn
> Still, *longing* for the dawn, *my son is growing* up
> *My son is* growing in her ocean
> *Our* love is like a *prop* in the ocean
> *Our* love is like a *prop* in the ocean
> Yahweh, Yahweh
> Always pain before *our* child is born

Yahweh, tell me now

With a vibration of the phone, Cliff sends a text:

MY DAD MOVED HIS QUEEN ON THE DIAGONAL TO H5 … HAD THE ATLANTIC CITY MAN IN CHECK MATE IN THREE MOVES… THE UNCOLORED MAN WITH SLICKED HAIR SHOULD'VE MOVED HIS PAWN FORWARD TWO PACES TO BLOCK THE QUEEN … INSTEAD HE MOVED INTO CHECKMATE… IN DISGUST HE FLIPPED OVER THE RAFT … THE CORAL PIECES FLOATED… DAD COLLECTED THE PIECES AND BOARD AND CLIMBED BACK ON THE CAPSIZED RAFT…

Back on our feet, we start wandering toward Philly, but suddenly we stop at the corner of the white concrete United States Post Office and Courthouse. We make a left onto Fourth Street. We follow the empty River LINE track and walk toward the back walls of the yellowish-brown brick prison. The jail is in our face, just one block away as we cross Arch Street.

Cliff sends another text. He sends the chess moves of his game with Ruby: dxe5 Bxe5

THE CHESS GAME

He sends another text: RUBY WANTS TO KNOW HOW YOUR GAME OF CHESS IS GOING?

Choker texts back: I CAN'T GO ON. I'LL GO ON as the River LINE rattles by us.

Cliff calls. "Bravo. The Samuel Beckett line."

"What?" Choker yells into the phone over the click-clacking. "The Shemaiah River LINE?"

THE CHESS GAME

Chapter 6

An empty newspaper honor box, with a bent bottom rack promoting an advertisement for Citizen's Funeral Home, stands alone on Federal Street. We stand a block away from it and the back of the Camden jail.

The metal box, just like us, is both empty and alone in the middle of this city.

"The prison plops a half of block in front of our *ways,*" Choker says with an odd, but equal mix of being trapped by annoyance and determination.

"Is that, the clink there, where we're going," Cresty says. "Should we just go back to City Hall and wait in safety under the clock until eight?"

"Go back? Like Pete's theory on Magnetic Reversion Reversal?" Choker asks. "Are we being pulled to the tower there because that is what we know, that is what we know as safe?"

"Na. Ya... like what pulls us all together eventually drives us apart

– the Magnetic Reversion," Cresty says. "We need to reverse the reversion and continue, to stay together."

There are three flagpoles in the courtyard, but we can only see the top half of the poles as a 10-foot high wall with barbed wire surrounds the prison.

"You would *not* think the king would be at a jail," Choker says with a definitiveness of just making a move into checkmate, or understanding Magnetic Reversion Reversal. "Not like The Three Mayors of Camden in jail, the king wouldn't be locked up."

"Isn't using The Three Mayors of Camden in jail a bit much? And you mean the Wizard, not the king," Cresty says criticizes and then corrects. She points to the three flagpoles one-by-one and says to Choker, "And who knows… maybe, bro."

Looking at the stained yellowish-brown bricks of the jail rising into the sunny sky, with no tall buildings behind it to the south, just free-floating clouds, we stand on the corner of Fourth and Arch, a small side street that runs into the Fire Administration back parking lot. There is a single gas pump, presumably for use by the fire administrators, connected by its hose to a Majestic Oil tanker truck.

"Let's wait," Choker says with his eyes perched on the gas pump.

"Wait?"

"Wait, yeah, for the oil truck to pull out. I want to spread some of the petro on the soles of my boots."

"What for?" Cresty asks plainly, or simply as if Choker didn't say, suggest, doing something crazy.

"Well, Pete told me on one of those days at the courts while waiting for *winners,* like learning on the steps of the Parthenon from Socrates himself…"

"You mean Hippocrates," Cresty injects as Choker continues, "That, Pete, on the way to his college roommate's wedding, one of the Lids, he stepped into what he thought must have been a 'gasoline spillage' in the parking lot of St. Mary of The Lakes in Medford.

"He never told you this?"

Cresty says only, "Go on."

"A few minutes later, he, Pete, walked up the aisle before the service, the mass, started to wish the groom luck, one of the Lids, you know the Leftover Intellectual Dumb *Sheeets.*"

"Of course, dumbass, it has only been a year away from them, but I will never forget them, the Lids," she says wrapping her arms around me. "My hope, my prayer is we all get tight again."

"Well, this might help the cause," Choker continues while looking at the oil truck, "the soles, Pete's boots, the black soles, started dissolving… he made black footprints behind him, as he walked up the white rolled out carpet that was stretched up the center aisle of the church.

"The other groomsmen had to roll up the white carpet, only seconds before the organ music started and the bride walked up the aisle… on the red church carpet. Pete put his shoes in the holy water basin, the one at the side entrance near the altar, to 'dissolve the devil' on his shoes. He had to stand on the elevated altar in his white basketball socks as the soles of his dressy black shoes continued to dissolve."

"Of course. Yeah, I remember the story," Cresty says in an unamused tone. "The groom, one of the Lids, was really hung over. His uncle was the priest, who allowed… advised his nephew to sit down on the altar… to take a timeout for a few minutes before taking the vows."

"So? Tell me… the correlation. Please."

"Well, you will like my thinking, as I'm looking out for you, with the *disolvement* of my kicks, this way my footprints will be left across the city as we look for the king."

"You mean the Wizard. And why is your ego so big that you want to leave footprints across the city? Especially dirty footprints like the arrested The Three Mayors. You want to leave clean footprints that people can't see but can feel, since they make a difference. Footprints that make a

THE CHESS GAME

difference, like the ones The Three Monsignors left, are leaving."

"Man, you're digging deep... and that's a grim, and maybe unfair comparison to The Three Mayors," Choker snaps. "I'm talking footprints, real ones, like leaving crumbs. As in Hansel and Gretel, so we can follow our footsteps back. So we always know where we are."

"*Dood*, as Pete would say, you have bread crumbs for a brain," Cresty chides. "All we have to do is look up and see the clock tower of City Hall to know where we are... where we came from... where we are going."

"No. I'm waiting," Choker says, turning into the fire administration parking lot, "I'm waiting... for the oil truck to pull out."

Cresty marches on. Alone. Well, with me. She crosses Fourth Street and turns the corner onto Federal Street where another magnificent bank building dominates the block. The bank is square and powerful in appearance, with gray granite blocks spread around the base six feet high. There, the stone turns white and with high arching windows reaching to the roof. The architecture, its side columns, is a rip-off, a knock-off rather, of the Parthenon. The building stands empty, like the Greek structure on the mound of the Acropolis.

The front entryway is also arched. It houses a golden double-door steel structure that looks like it took four people to open, back when the bank was in business. The impressive entrance is one just one step up from the sidewalk.

On the steps, which are just wide enough for a person to lie down, is an apparently middle-aged lady bundled up in a camouflage jacket. She has a gray sleeping bag that matches the concrete of the building wrapped around her legs. Her head rests against a thin, long, blue bag, which hangs from the golden knob of the door.

"Sorry," she says to Cresty, who is leaning up against the front pillar.

Cresty jumps. "Sorry, I didn't see you there," Cresty says startled. "Don't mean to alarm ya."

Cresty looks away and then up above the magnificent arched doorway. She reads the chiseled inscription.

"Sorry about invading your space here at the old Central Trust Company," Cresty says while still looking up, reading.

"Why would you be sorry?" the lady says. "It was built in 1899 and was added to the National Register of Historic Places."

"I'm standing in the doorway of history," Cresty says smiling.

THE CHESS GAME

"No, I'm sorry you are here," the lady says with gentle sincerity, not getting her joke. "What floor is your man on? Mine is on the seventh. He is easy to spot since the lucky 7th is just one floor from the top. You can see his head in the slot window by the inside corner. The one, the handsome one, with the camo-green hat."

His hat is really more riverweed brown than camouflage green.

"We look at each other all day," the lady continues. "And we sleep next to each other all night. Sorry I don't have room for you on the stoop. I can't get up and leave, or else someone will lie down in my... home. Except when it first gets dark out. That's when I scramble to find food, usually in the trash can outside Hank's Place on Market. They, that is, someone else would try to take my stoop even with my sleeping bag here and my lucky bag hanging on the doorknob both clearly and definitively marking my spot... can't trust anyone... not even here at the Central *Trust* Company.

"What floor is your man on?"

Across the street, the middle-aged man wearing the L.L. Bean tan vest jacket without sleeves, the one we first saw walk out from under the 676 overpass, walks from around the corner of an alley between the prison and the old city library, another fine looking building like this bank here.

He has wrapped the green stripped-sleeve turtleneck around his waist like Cresty did with her hooded gray Ursinus College sweat shirt. The man with the mirror sunglasses wearing the Abe Lincoln black stovepipe top hat is pushing the empty shopping cart. While leaning on the shopping cart, he pulls out from inside his vest the cardboard sign: "the Wizard will fix everything."

The Majestic Oil truck tanker turns the corner and chugs up Federal. Even with the trucks transition spinning loudly before clicking into third gear, we are able to hear a basketball bouncing inside the prison courtyard. A player calls a foul. "Ball, man!" Suddenly the ball bounces over the barbed-wire wall and in one-hop it lands in the shopping cart of the man behind the mirror sunglasses. He seems to be staring at us, Cresty and me.

He follows us down Federal Street, toward the river and away from the tower, pushing the cart along the prison wall. As if we're going to fake him out, or lose him, we briskly turn the corner on Fourth and pick up our pace even more toward the Fire Administration building. We stop by an abandoned TV on the corner of Fourth and Arch.

THE CHESS GAME

We are hoping he continues down Federal to the river. If he turns downs Fourth, we will let him pass, thinks Cresty, as we see Choker bend over by the gas pump. But the Abe Lincoln hat man with the sign stops at a lime green fire hydrant on Federal, near the empty newspaper honor box with a bent bottom rack. He leans his cardboard sign over the advertisement for Citizen's Funeral Home so we can read the red letters. Again we read: "the Wizard will fix everything."

The lady in the camouflage jacket pokes her head around the Central Trust Company and yells, "Do you know him?"

"Who?"

"Who?" the lady asks incredulously. "Who do you think? There... Romeo over there ... yeah Romeo."

Cresty yells nervously back, "Oh, Romero you mean?" She reaches into her number 24 jersey and pulls out the paperback.

"Says here, right here in the official church pamphlet, that Oscar Romero was jailed when he was 26..." Cresty yells even more nervously, turning to look, probably to see if Choker is done gassing up his soles.

"In 1943, he was called home from Rome where he was doing doctoral work and he stopped in Cuba where he was detained for coming from Fascist Italy," Cresty screams.

The middle-aged man with the mirror sunglasses wearing an Abe Lincoln black stovepipe top hat slides the sign inside his L. L. Bean vest as he begins to cross the street toward us. He throws the basketball at us. Suddenly, from behind us, Choker slips, diving as he catches the ball. The gas from the bottom of his thick-soled hiking boots doesn't leave footprints, but it leaves an oily smear on the ball. The name "Howard Unruh" seems to be scribbled on the ball.

Choker calls Ruby. The sign man stops in the middle of Federal Street. He pulls tight on the Abe Lincoln hat as if he is strapping on a football helmet and ready to charge us.

"Who… hey my man Ruby Red…" Choker says nervously like Cresty was speaking, before sounding suddenly relaxed, "Who… is Howard Unruh?"

"Yabba, dabba Busta, Howard took'd the Walk of Death, too, like youse," Ruby says. "Back in 1949. During a 12-minute wander through his neighborhood, he shot'd and killed 13 people. He was locked up in the jail there, the other tower, for 60 years. He didn't talk to anyone. He just shot'd baskets outside all day by himself.

"He died *fer* years ago, Ruby thinks... yeah, turned in back in 2009... is that *fer* years ago already? Yup, this is 2015, right?"

"So, he isn't still shooting. Shooting baskets, I mean," Choker asks. "I'm holding a basketball with his scribbled name... but it's clear enough to make out."

"Yup, youse'd be at the jail then," Ruby continues. "Unruh's rank was a tank soldier during World War II. He kept notes on every German he killed. Interesting, huh? He fought in the Battle of the Bulge. He shot'd his unfortunate 13 in Camden using a German luger pistol."

Cliff talks into the speakerphone

"That's all, 12 minutes," Cliffs says. "The USS Indy sunk during the second Great War, when just after midnight on July 30, her starboard side met two of her Emperor's torpedoes... she listed to the bow.

"Twelve minutes later, she rolled over and her stern rose to heaven and she plunged.

"About 300 went down with her in a dozen minutes," Cliff says like reading textbook.

"Twelve minutes," Ruby says, "just like Unruh's Walk of Death."

"Twelve minutes is all some *ways* takes," Cliff says.

"Like Ruby winning."

"Winning?" Cliff laughs. "You mean, of course, winning again... winning in this chess game."

"You mean the Game of Chess," Ruby spits into the phone.

Cliff says: "Nxe5." Ruby immediately responds: "Nxe5."

With a sudden burst of needed courage, we start to wander toward the sign man standing in the middle of the street. But, we hesitate. Still, he backs up so Choker and Cresty sit down at the corner bank across from the prison walls. Pushing an empty stroller, another woman walks up to the lady laying on the bank stoop. Smiling, she holds her little kid's hand and with the other hand waves up to the slotted window. A hand in the window points to the clock on the City Hall tower, which says its 11:12... but is an hour behind.

"I will play that number tonight in the Pick Six – 11 and 12 and then 13 - for good luck," the lady says hopefully, not knowing she should really play 12:12... and probably not knowing that 12 wasn't really a lucky number in Camden in 1949 or in the South Pacific in 1945.

Choker sings Sunday Bloody Sunday as he stands up and again walks across the street toward the man with the shopping cart. Choker is dribbling the basketball.

The Majestic Oil truck tanker backs up on the one-way street between Choker and the sign man. The transmission doesn't skip in reverse. The truck turns smoothly and backs gently onto Fourth Street.

The man doesn't disappear. We can still read the letters on his L.L. Bean vest. Slowly, with uneven steps, Choker edges close enough to reach him... to pull off easily his mirror sunglasses, to knock off his Abe Lincoln black stovepipe top hat...

Swiftly, the man lifts and holds the sign over his face... Choker tries to hand, no shove the man the ball ... but he slips again when his oily boots step onto the curb ... the man pushes the cart with force and speeds around the corner.

Using his hands as crutches, Choker slides onto the curb. We are all watching him, the man, push the cart until we can only hear the squeaking wheels. Choker does not pursue him for some reason. Well, because of the obvious. Maybe because he slapped gas on his soles.

He slides back across Federal Street. We all sit on the curb of the empty street slicked by oil. Looking toward the river, perhaps for comfort, we can see the towering skyscrapers of Philadelphia behind the aquarium's half dome. The aquarium is bustling with business as school kids wait in line holding their mom's hands. They lean up with their backpacks up against the building filled with sea life.

    Gurgling and clearing his throat, Choker stands and sings U2's Sunday, Bloody Sunday. He is marching his feet to the music and faking to hold a flag:

> Yes...
> I can't believe the news *you say*
> Oh, I can't close my eyes
> And make it go away
> How long...
> How long must we sing this song
> How long, how long...
> 'cause tonight... we can be as one
> Tonight...
> Broken bottles under children's feet
> Bodies strewn across the *Camden* street
> But I won't heed the battle call
> It puts my back up
> Puts my back up against *city hall*
> *Today, Bloody Today*
> *Today, Bloody Today*
> *Today, Bloody Today*

THE CHESS GAME

Rubbing Choker's strong shoulders, now tense, Cresty says to him how the song isn't about fighting but surrendering.

"Surrender, in both the political and religious sense, and especially in the spiritual sense if religion isn't someone's formal gig," she says. "Surrender…"

Choker, though, keeps singing… and marching:

> And the battle's just begun
> There's many lost, but tell *us* who has won
> The trench is dug within our hearts
> And mothers, children, brothers, sisters
> Torn apart
> *Today, Bloody Today*
> *Today, Bloody Today*

"Really, bro," Cresty injects again, "when Bono runs and bounces and marches around onstage with a white flag singing Bloody Sunday, well he is saying, really singing, this… to surrender… not only about politics and government, but also about the big f-word… faith, to surrender to God."

"Surrender, never, to the man," Choker declares, "perhaps to God, yeah." Taking a big

Bono marching step, his right foot slides. He continues to sing to his iPhone's music:

> How long...
> How long must we sing this song
> How long, how long...
> 'cause tonight...we can be as one
> *Today*... tonight...
> *Today, Bloody Today*
> *Today, Bloody Today*

    The lady in the camouflage jacket invites us to sit on the stoop with her. She slides over, spreading out her sleeping bag as padding for all of us.
    On his phone, Choker turns off the pause on Bloody Sunday and sings:

> Wipe the tears from your eyes
> Wipe your *fears* away
> Oh, wipe your tears away
> Oh, wipe your *fears* away
> *Today, Bloody Today*
> Oh, wipe your blood shot eyes
> *Today, Bloody Today*
> *Today, Bloody Today*
> *Today, Bloody Today*

THE CHESS GAME

My mom is thinking that the lady looks a lot like the nice nurse from the pediatrician's office she visited when she was a kid. Her dad, Pete, took her over the river to here, Camden, from Drexel Hill, to visit a specialist doc.

Pete told her that Camden High, the school, was called The Castle on The Hill. He told her back then, in the mid-2000's, Camden wasn't any Acropolis, what the Greeks called "The City in the Sky." Pete said Camden wasn't even "The City on the Hill" ... not like the high school and its great *baskaball* teams.

The lady sings with Choker. She removes a violin from her blue bag that is hanging on the door knob and plays along, singing:

> And it's true we are immune
> When fact is fiction and TV reality
> And today the *cities* cry
> We eat and drink while tomorrow they die
> The real battle just begun
> To claim the victory Jesus won
> *Oh...*
> *Today, Bloody Today*
> *Today, Bloody Today*

Across the street, the L. L. Bean vest man with the mirror sunglasses, wearing the Abe Lincoln black stovepipe top hat reappears as if he just dropped in from a tower.

"You know," she says, "His great, great, great grand daddy shot the man who shot Lincoln?"

"We heard," Cresty says.

"Yeah, shot John Wilkes Booth," the lady says, playing an eerie note on her violin. "Then he moved to Camden... brought bad luck with him here."

We slowly get up, say goodbye to the lady with the violin, and walk after the man with the shopping cart. But he scoots away down the alley between the jail and the city library.

The Camden public library has books on its shelves that we can see through the dusty front windows. The front door is barricaded with a sign: NO TRESPASSING

THE CHESS GAME

Chapter 7

A yellow, crumpled newspaper twirls in the wind, blowing aimlessly, like a tumbleweed in Tombstone, when the back gate opens to the prison and a W.B. Mason delivery truck peels out. Without slowing, not breaking stride, barely missing being run over, a girl dressed in all black with white headphones dangling from her ears appears to be chatting into her phone… but no… she is making no sounds. No words.

The balled sheet of newspaper dances across Federal Street, bounces down the block and then whips back across the street. The drifting tumbleweed paper ball flattens up against the metal black fence surrounding a freshly paved parking lot between two new, well, modern office buildings. The newspaper flies away again, tightening into a half-wrapped ball and bounces free, floating in the wind.

Two Camden Iron & Metal flatbed trucks turn the corner sharply on Fourth and Federal, forcing a postman, who looks like he isn't many years from retirement, to step back onto the sidewalk – twice.

Even with his scratched glasses sliding down his nose, the man delivering the mail wears a smile and happy eyes. He seems unaffected even though he was twice nearly run down by two trucks from the same company.

"Missed me again," he yells at the speeding trucks as he safely crosses Federal Street. "Still too quick for you slow guys, you duds."

He readjusts the sagging, but flat mailbag on his shoulder. He reaches into his bag, pulls out a paper advertisement circular, wipes the tops of his black polished shiny shoes, rolls up the paper into a ball and throws it like a baseball across the street toward us.

Now, two balls of paper bounce together in the light wind.

"Ironic," the postman yells from across the street while pointing to the two newspapers now pinned against the fence. "My dad was a mailman in the fifties here and he said that empty lot there housed the city newspaper, the Courier-Post, and that was his main drop of mail each day.

"Now, right there at 132 Federal Street, a new empty parking lot flanks the sides of two new buildings waiting for some business dot.com startup types to move in. I still deliver my air-ball papers each day in my dad's honor.

"Ironic, too how my floating newspaper deliveries can't even get through the fence and dance on its former homeland. The Courier-Post

THE CHESS GAME

abandoned the city it wrote most of its stories about. Left, too. Split. Gone like the two iron trucks.

"The city newspaper moved to the suburbs, into Cherry Hill, supporting the *white flight* before anyone in City Hall knew there was one."

Slipping and then sliding, Choker runs into the street. He reaches for the one newspaper ball that is blowing free. The wind blows the paper between the spokes of the fence. He climbs the fence. Running in circles, trying to catch the sphere, he falls on it.

Out of breath, he leans on the fence with the paper ball in his hand. He spikes it on top of one of the pointed spokes. Cresty and I cross Federal Street halfway between the prison and the river.

"You would *not* think the king would be here either, not at an empty lot where a newspaper building once stood," Choker whispers to us when we step onto the curb.

"You mean the Wizard," Cresty whispers back.

The clock on the City Hall tower strikes 12 noon... even though it is an hour behind.

"I should be in the newspaper," Choker yells at the city hall clock, or maybe just the skies. No. He is yelling toward the clock. "I should be playing big time college basketball... I should be written up in the sports section like my dad was back in the 80's. As my dad says, "That's when life was as good as a Larry Bird jump shot."

Reflecting, Cresty is thinking how Choker's last name is Byrd.

"The 80's, that's when my dad moved to nearby Merchantville in the suburbs," the postman says, still on the other side of Federal Street, turning toward City Hall. "As kids in Camden, we played ball on Friday nights at the Merchantville gym… until the wall nearest the playground cracked.

"We moved to Merchantville because the library there in town, on Center Street was open… unlike in Camden."

From behind us, we hear the rattling wheels, the squeaking of a … the shopping cart.

"I once played the game and lived in a house in the suburbs," the homeless man wearing the mirror sunglasses and the Abe Lincoln black stovepipe top hat, and pushing the shopping cart yells. He is in the middle of the fenced in parking lot, where the newspaper once was printed and reported the news of the day. "But I was pulled back to live where my great, great, great granddaddy lived on 308 Mechanic Street and below South 4th Street on Pine Street… but the houses were boarded up… with all

THE CHESS GAME

the people on the streets, how can they board up houses?

"How can they, the government, board up the house of Boston Corbett?"

The shopping cart gains speed toward Choker. The man in the L.L. Bean vest swerves and just misses him before stopping. With his head still down and his Abe Lincoln black stovepipe top hat pointing ahead, he opens the unlocked fence gate. He slams the gate leaving Choker inside and Cresty outside with him.

A lady driver with a male passenger stops a small gray car in the middle of Federal Street. The car idles between us and the homeless looking man pushing the shopping cart, and the postman across the street.

"Sir," she says to the postman, "Where is the Hall of Justice?"

"Just Google map it," the postman says, adjusting the shoulder strap on his bag.

The shopping cart man yells to the lady, "Just keep going up Federal Street and make a right at the light, go down one block and the modern brown brick building is the Hall of Justice. You can't miss it … no it is right there. Justice is… there… like in the pistol of my great, great, great granddaddy."

Suddenly, lowering his voice to a solemn tone,

squeezing the handlebar of the shopping cart, the man says, "Good luck… or Johnny Luckett …"

The man on the passenger side begins to roll up the window as he rolls his eyes and says, "Yeah, oh yeah, Johnny Luckett… justice."

"Justice is in the eye of the beholder," the shopping cart man says in a pained voice. He is looking down, allowing the passenger to see his reflection in the mirror sunglasses. "But ya'll get a fair shake. The law is fair. Firm but fair now here in Camden.

"Remember the law is trying to protect you, too … sometimes though, Big Brother tries to help us too much instead of let us be… to much help, giving ain't no good either.

"Not enough shopping carts for all the people, you see."

The passenger swipes the shopping cart man's mirror sunglasses off his face just as Cliff calls on the cell. Choker pulls out his phone while Cresty dips down, acting like she is trying to pick up the balled newspaper rolling around at her feet, but looking up to sneak a glance at the shopping cart man's face as he lowers his Abe Lincoln black stovepipe top hat over his eyes and scrambles to pick up his mirror sunglasses.

THE CHESS GAME

"Don't rat me out, people still hate the blood of the man who shot the man who shot Lincoln," the homeless looking, shopping cart man orders Cresty, putting on his mirror sunglasses and pushing his cart across the street. "Don't look for... me... you will never... find the Wizard."

Cresty is frozen.

"I need to find, I'm trying to find my own self-worth, my identity again," Choker says to him as he fumbles to answer his phone that keeps chiming to the U2 song "Bad."

"I need to find my voice in this world."

The phone stops ringing as we watch the homeless looking man push his cart down Fourth Street to Arch Street. We don't chase him. He looks both ways twice before sitting down on the abandoned TV on the corner across from the fire administration gas pump.

"Bad" rings out again.

"Answer the phone," Cresty demands," it could be Siri, your spiritual advisor."

Cliff speaks:

"The sailors of the USS Indy floundered in the water for four days before being rescued," Cliff says. "Four days of feeding for the sharks... the Navy had a fleet in the South Pacific and it took four days before a search plane spotted hundreds of its men serving as shark bait."

Cliff huffs into the speakerphone and then says his chess move: "Bb3." And Ruby says, "Ne7... I like moving Ruby's knight during the day."

Laughing, Ruby adds, "You know that Number seven jersey could be referring to the Holy Book. That's what Ruby says anyway. "I'd like to move Ruby's knight to space seven, too, cause the Bible is divided into seven sections.

"The perfection of God. That's reflected in Number Seven, so says Ruby."

"Is that another hint for the chess piece? Cresty asks. "Is the move to space seven... should we make the same move?"

"The city made its move back in 2000," Ruby says. "The Republican National Convention came to Philadelphia and many of the delegates were planning on staying across the river in the burbs, in the Cherry Hill hotels, near where the Garden State Racetrack once raced."

Ruby pauses. It sounds like he is stomping his feet.

"But," he continues, the thumping stopped, "the only way to get to the suburbs from Philadelphia was by taking the Admiral Wilson Boulevard, which splits downtown Camden from the East

THE CHESS GAME

Side. However, the boulevard was lined with unsightly, sleazy strip joints.

"So the strip joints were torn down and today there is just land, no businesses. Just empty green space with weeds sprouting between the gated barriers to keep cars out. No business grew there. The hookers even left the empty strip..."

As Ruby's voice fades, with a thoughtless swipe, Choker's phone switches to more U2 music and he sings Acrobat:

> Don't believe what you *fear*
> Don't believe what *is free*
> If you just close your eyes
> You can *join* the enemy
> When I first met you girl
> *We* had fire in *our* soul
> What happened *our* face of melting in snow?
> Now it looks like this
> And *we be shallow*
> Or *we* can *split*
> *We* can throw it *out*
> Or *Choker* it
> And you can *scream*
> So *scream* out loud
> You know that *our* time is coming *unbound*

So don't let the *blowhards* grind you down
No, nothing makes sense

    Holding… rubbing me, Cresty says, "Indeed, Choke, nothing makes sense."
    "Well," Choker says, "you must have your *ways* for sense to be made."
    "Indeed, *ways*," Cresty says, "is all we have."
    Kneeling on his right knee, Choker continues singing:

Nothing seems to fit
I know *we'd* hit out
If *we* only knew who to hit
And *we'd* join the movement
If there was one *we* could believe in
Yeah *we'd* break *heads* and wine
If there was a church I could *grieve* in
'Cause *we* need *to sow*
To *break* the cup
To *suck* it up
To *bring a glow*
We can't let *right* go
I must be an *autocrat*
To talk like this
And act like that
And *we* can *scream*

THE CHESS GAME

> So *scream* out loud
> And don't let the *blowhards* grind *us* down

Slapping her arm around Choker's shoulders, tugging on his slumping neck, Cresty sings, mimicking Choker, "The bastards will grind you down, like they did to Pete."

"That's why," Choker injects, "you must have your *ways*."

"Yup, w*ays*," Cresty agrees, "*ways* is all we have."

Pulling her arm tighter around his neck, Choker continues singing:

> Oh, *hurt*, hurts baby
> What are we going to do? Now it's all been said
> No new ideas *in courthouse* and every *word* has been *said*
> And I must be an *autocrat*
> To talk like this
> And act like that
> And you can *scream*
> So *scream* out loud
> And *we* can find
> *Our* own way out
> And *we* can build

And *up our* will
And *we* can *fall*
We can't wait until
We need cash
Can't buy a sneeze
Responsibilities
And *we* can *shove*
But *can we* love
And *we* know that the tide is *making sound*
So don't let the *blowhards* grind *us* down

Waving her fingers in front of her as if to say no, Cresty puts her hand over the phone. Protesting, she says Bono is singing about hypocrisy, quoting the Irish singer: "I must be an acrobat to talk like this and act like that."

Cresty rubs her belly. She glances at her pamphlet.

"Oscar Romero used radio sermons to get out his message," Cresty says after a few seconds. "Bono uses his music. The same message. Social injustice. Liberation justice."

"No one listens to the radio anymore," Choker says as one of the flying pieces of newspaper unwraps from a ball and pins up around his right foot, over his untied hiking boot with the thick sole.

THE CHESS GAME

Doctor Knight, the anesthesiologist doc who walked one block down to the chess game, is now walking past the prison and toward us. He is being followed by Wali, the parking garage attendant.

Doc and Wali stop when they see us. They wave to the homeless looking man in the L. L. Bean vest sitting on the TV down Fourth Street with his feet up on the empty shopping cart. He adjusts his mirror sunglasses and Abe Lincoln black stovepipe top hat and pulls out his sign from his vest: "The Wizard will fix everything."

"Who is he?" Choker asks Doc and Wali.

"We practiced Vendetta Yoga together when I lived in Tent City," Doc says, projecting his right shoulder toward his ear with an awkward wiggle. "I now live on a house boat in Wiggins Park. Well, not the park, but the Marina… I moved out when he never delivered George Washington's tent… that he promised… for me to use."

"You did." Choker asks.

"Yeah, I thought Vendetta would loosen up my shoulder. The shoulder doc said I need it replaced, but that I'm too young. He said they only last 10 years. I told the doc that I wouldn't live 10 years… not like this… not here. He said, 'hell, you're only 51.' "

"Na Doc. The man with shopping cart," Cresty

explains without any annoyance. "Choker is asking if you lived with him."

"Yup. The man with the mirror sunglasses," Choker agrees quickly, raising his curled hands to his eyes, mimicking sunglasses.

"The homeless looking man across the street told me, ordered us 'don't rat me out,'" Cresty says.

"Don't," Doc says. "Did you notice he is wearing an Abe Lincoln black stovepipe top hat?"

Choker and Cresty look at each other in bewilderment. "Notice," Cresty says incredulously and then they both nod in agreement.

"It's Abe's hat," the Doc says. "He wears the sunglasses to hide from Booth's Avengers."

Wali nods.

"He also warned me, 'don't look for… I guess the Wizard… you will never find, I guess, the Wizard.'" Choker says.

"You won't," Wali says. "And don't you mean, the king, Ruby's king?"

Doc nods.

"I only told him how I needed to find, I'm trying to find my own self-worth, my identity again," Choker says. "I said I 'need to find my voice in this world.'"

"You need to find only your heart again,"

Cresty says. "Find your heart like how Pete helped you find it on the courts of Avalon and the bars of Sea Isle.

"What are you looking to find down here Doc?" Cresty asks.

"Doing the Vendetta was much harder than just taking pain pills, which killed my marriage but helped my shoulder," Doc confesses. "I was afraid to stop.

"The pain pills helped my wife at first, too. The pills were plenty in the hospital, especially for an anesthesiologist. I would take pills from the patients' rooms and bring home the poppers to her, to help mediate, for the pain of losing babies… one in a miscarriage.

I just need to find my courage again to go on … I still can't sleep."

Wali puts his arm around Doc and says, "Why don't you try counting sheep."

Doc makes two fists.

"That's the *ways*, not easy to find courage Doc, especially down here in Camden where you need to be fearless to survive when your courage runs scared," Wali says, making two fists back at the Doc as if they are going to square off. "At least you are smart. I'm just a d-d-dumb, dumbass parking attendant going **nowhere in a flash**."

"Well, where you going now?" asking Cresty.

"I'm just going down to the USS New Jersey, I volunteer on my lunch break, trying to learn, trying to develop a brain," he says. "And, volunteering helps eliminate the paws of Big Brother."

THE CHESS GAME

Chapter 8

With the heat of the sun baking the black tar roofs of the falling and failing row homes of Camden and searing the oily asphalt of the potholed streets, a shiny sailboat putts down the river under the power of its quiet and efficient diesel engine.

The entire city begins to stink like the petroleum-slicked soles of Choker's hiking boots. The breeze coming off the river protects the captain and his mistress sailing thoughtlessly from the smell, pushing back the trapped odor around the tardy clock tower and up over City Hall.

Our wandering pace has switched into speed walking north up Third Street, away from the man behind the mirror sunglasses, wearing the Abe Lincoln black stovepipe top hat. The squeak of the shopping cart is only in our fears. We are headed opposite of the unconcerned sailboat and back toward the Ben Franklin Bridge. We aren't on a stroll anymore.

Are we in a chamber? We feel like we're in a tunnel since the back of the L3 Communications building borders up to Third Street with no entrance or windows on the first floor. There are only a few tinted windows on the second and third floors, as if there are secrets inside.

The L3 back wall is built of attractive reddish-pink stonework, highlighted by white trim blocks for the length of the block. The entrance to the engineering facility is on the side of the river facing another L3 building that is separated by a smoothly paved asphalt parking lot. The admittance to the L3 buildings is only through this guarded parking lot. Only workers are allowed. The building is a great wall, blocking out the world... but not the smell of the burning tar row home roofs surrounding the intellectual fortress.

"I heard from a college friend, I forget her name, she was on the team, too, but her uncle has a friend whose neighbor works in there," Cresty says pausing and then pointing with her thumb like a hitchhiker at the back wall, "that there is where they build bombs that don't explode, magnetic bombs that knock out information systems. Do you think, Choke, they have bottles of water in there. Could you fetch me a drop leftover from a champagne glass in there?"

Taking our last few steps on the matching stone pavers, we slow down our Olympic speed-walking pace near the end of the wall. Choker looks behind us and then peeks his head out around the corner of the wall.

THE CHESS GAME

"All clear," he says.

Cresty sighs. "Any water?"

"Not even magnetic bombs," Choker quips while grabbing her hand, pulling her to keep pace.

"How would we know?"

Relieved, turning the corner, we see a pile of otherwise lonesome leaves swirl around another crumpled up sheet of newspaper. The whirlwind in the tunnel made by the L# buildings makes this a captivating circle for our eyes. We walk toward the river on Market Street on the reddish-pink pavers that match the L3 building's pavers while keeping our eyes on the swirling newspaper.

We can see the man in the black hoodie get up from the bank bench on the other side of the street and pluck a plastic white trash bag that is tied at the top out of a black metal trashcan in front of Hank's Restaurant.

At the L3 building closest to the river, we dart across Market to the back of the Victor.

We seemed to have somehow walked in a circle. Actually, we did.

"Unless the king is on wheels and is following us, we aren't going to find him making loops," Choker laments. "We're back under Nipper the Dog."

"You mean the Wizard," Cresty says. "And the

Wizard could be a *her* and not a *him*."

We are back to wandering at our wandering pace.

With slow steps, we meander on the other side of Market Street, back toward the clock on City Hall.

Two men in yellow jackets, with the slogan KEEPING CAMDEN CLEAN AND SAFE in black letters on the bottom of their back, are pushing yellow trashcans on wheels. The one man has the name "Caesar" stitched on his jacket's front chest pocket.

They both stare at the newspaper ball blowing around, playing a fool to and with the wind, as if the two men are hypnotized. Caesar is eating a Slim Jim. He says to the other cleaning man, "Caesar is asking you if you want a bite?" while he stabs the paper with a pointed poker. Scraping the poker along the inside of the can, Caesar drops the trash in the bucket as he says to his partner who hasn't picked up any trash and doesn't want a bite of his snack, "What do I look like... an ass-wiping enabler?"

We stand on Market Street where the blue dumpster is now empty and the support poles in the opening between the two row homes are now gone. There is an open plot of land flanked by two sides of row homes. Or are they businesses?

Two hitchhikers stand under a tree in front of the empty lot where a home with a family once stood. Or maybe a business that once fed families. The hitchhiker, the one without the Yankees hat, sticks his thumb out. The small, circular fallen leaves left from the winter surround the other man in the Yankees cap, the one who is wearing sneakers without laces. The leaves look like used condoms.

"Just got released from the Big House," the hitchhiker without the hat says to us. "Walked to the river, saw the dog on the tower, don't know where to go… where to start."

"When Oscar Romero was released from prison in Cuba, he sailed to Mexico and then travelled to San Salvador," Cresty says aloud, but specifically to him. "He was assigned to Our Lady of Peace."

"Are you," the hitchhiker without the Yankees hat says to us, "following a similar path… to peace."

"Ya. Perhaps. Na. Perhaps," Cresty answers him.

"Why don't you go to the Romero Center on the East Side of Camden," she continues, now preaching and looking at him. "Ask for Monsignor McDermott. He found the path to peace by returning to his God-forgotten neighborhood…

God forgot the neighborhood or the neighborhood forgot God?" he asks in a perplexed tone as Cresty finishes saying, "and brought back God to the people… his people."

"I will go where the wind of the Great Spirit takes me," the hitchhiker without the hat says. "Like that balled up newspaper that was blowing around. I got no *ways* else to go."

"But… in life," Choker says, "you must have your *ways*."

"Yeah, w*ays*," Cresty adds, "*ways* is all we have."

The two hitchhikers split. The one without the hat walks north toward the Ben Franklin Bridge. The one with the Yankees hat, now on sideways, walks closer toward us.

"Hey. I'm a Yankees fan, too," Choker says to him… the hat-wearing hitchhiker who must be in a daze from just getting released from jail.

"Ya. We're both big Derek Jeter fans," Cresty says to the blank faced man with the tilted hat, the one without the deep thoughts.

"Je-ter … De-rek … Je-ter," Choker chants as the man continues walking… walks by us with a blank-stoned-dazed face and without saying a word.

THE CHESS GAME

"The Zombie apocalypse came just in time for lunch," Cresty says. "Hope they bring some water."

"Hope they pass the wine," Choker says.

The two men in yellow jackets and yellow trashcans on wheels roll up on us. Their wheels don't squeak. The one with the name "Caesar" stitched on his jacket's front chest pocket starts stabbing at the condom-looking dead leaves and drops them one-by-one in the bucket.

The one hitchhiker without the hat walks back toward us, away from the Ben Franklin Bridge. He doesn't act like a Zombie, not like the other hitchhiker, but he could be faking, of course.

"I walked to the bridge, but a man pushing a shopping cart told me not to go past the bridge into North Camden," the hitchhiker said. "He called it the Forbidden Territory."

"Was he wearing his mirror sunglasses?" Cresty asks.

"I forget," he says. "I told him I saw the church steeple and I wanted to go there to find my ways again, but the man said the church closed years ago. He said there are no churches left in the Forbidden Territory on the other side of the Ben Franklin Bridge."

"Man, Ben Franklin himself would be bummed," Choker says. "I know from studying

American History last year at Ursinus that Franklin preached and campaigned for Colonial unity.

"Which way, what road did the unity take out of town?"

"I have no ways," the hitchhiker laments again.

"Oscar Romero didn't have any *ways* to go either," Cresty says to him. "He became director of the archdiocese newspaper. He defended the traditional teachings of the Catholic Church.

"He defined his ways for the world. For Monsignor McDermott. For us. Teachings, too, drip like blood, to be sucked by life… not for the zombies."

We follow the hitchhiker back down Market Street toward the river.

A shiny new silver car with a dented front bumper and a cracked right head light pulls out of the gated parking lot of the Nipper building. The expensive sedan makes a left, going the wrong way on one-way Front Street that divides the luxury lofts from the an empty, bombed-out looking building across from the Victor that could pass for Zombie Headquarters.

"You see how the abandoned building is constructed with the same color red bricks of the refurbished Victor," the hitchhiker without the Yankees hat on sideways says, "But there are no

THE CHESS GAME

windows in the old structure, let alone the new green shiny metal ones like in its rebuilt neighboring one under the Nipper.

"When I was in jail, I stared out the slotted windows to Nipper the Dog and this abandoned building wondering how did one old factory get rebuilt and the other one get left to decay."

Lowering a sketching pad, a college student drawing the historic Nipper property says, "If you listen closely you can still hear Nipper and 'His Master's Voice' echoing from the tower stained glass windows.

"Listen…"

A Real estate lady, who is taking a picture of historic property with a real camera, not her phone, says, "Camden was the headquarters of the Victor Talking Machine Company. An unknown British artist painted the picture of his brother's dog sitting in front of a phonograph and listening… the picture made the Fox Terrier the most famous dog on the planet."

The hitchhiker injects, "But when RCA bought the Victor in 1929, the growing company removed the iconic four stained glass windows in the tower. RCA took down Nipper, too, in 1969.

"Huh? Man, what you say? That's confusing," Choker interrupts.

"Then, 10 years later, RCA made new stained-glass windows and replaced them," the real estate lady injects, nodding in agreement with the hitchhiker and looking at the photos on her camera. "The windows were damaged during the 80's, ruined through neglect after RCA was acquired by General Electric …

"And began developing intelligent systems," the hitchhiker injects again, "for the Government."

She studies us and asks, "Do you think I should include this historical information in my online narrative of the units for sale in the Victor? Do you think young people like you care?"

"I cared because I looked at the building every day," the hatless hitchhiker says. "Gots to go."

"Come back," the real estate lady pleads as the hitchhiker walks back toward the Ben Franklin Bridge. "Don't go. Not far anyway. I can get you a Sallie Mae or Freddie Mac mortgage… or is it Freddie Mae and Sallie Mac..."

"You need to let go," Choker says to her. "Did you ever hear the two monks on the mountain story?"

"Ya. He means the parable Pete told us. You want to tell her?" Cresty asks.

She watches the hitchhiker vanish into the shadow of the bridge as Choker nods and says:

THE CHESS GAME

"There are two monks walking in the Himalayan Mountains, they come up to a river, raging from the spring snow melt. They need to get across the river to get back to their Tibetan monastery. They look down at the angry river for a narrow spot to cross, but there isn't any, just a young lady with two water jugs. She's also trying to cross the river, to get the water back to her kids and the elderly in the village, but she can't get across."

Choker walks two fingers down to the end of the real estate lady's camera before saying in a low, serious voice, "So one monk walks down to the woman with the jugs, the water jugs, I mean, picks her up and carries her across the river.

"He, the monk, puts her down."

Choker takes her camera and emphatically puts it down on the ground. There is a crack. He takes his foot off a flattened Starbucks cup.

"After putting her down, he walks up the side of the river and meets up with the other monk, who crossed the river upstream on his own. They walk about a mile when the other monks says, 'you know as monks, we took a vow not only to never touch a woman, but never to look at one … yet you just went down river and picked one up, a woman… and carried her.'

"The one monk turns and says, 'True, Grasshopper, I carried her, but I put her down a mile ago… you're the one who is still carrying her.'"

Kicking the Starbucks cup, Choker flops on the ground next to the camera and sits in a Buddha position.

The real estate lady picks up her camera and asks, "Is that a true story?"

"True? Well… all but the Grasshopper part," Choker says. "I added Grasshopper to the true parable."

"True or false, this story never gets old," Cresty says. "That story has helped me so much in life. I don't know where Pete heard it, but it makes so much sense.

"You see, the monk couldn't leave the lady, the woman with the jugs, you know the jugs of water, there since her kids and family needed the water to live, but he had to break a vow to help the lady with the jugs… the jugs of water."

"Cute story, but the windows were replaced when the builder converted the lofts," the real estate lady says, shifting her thoughts back to the Victor. "I will include the new windows in the narrative. Do you think I should include how this Nipper Building is registered on the National

THE CHESS GAME

Register of Historic Places?"

The college student folds up her drawing of the historic property and says, "Remember if you listen closely you can still hear 'His Master's Voice' and then she nudges real close to Choker and whispers, "if you listen closely you can still hear ...

"RUFF! RUFF! RUFF!"

Choker jumps back as the artist girl laughs wildly after barking in his ear. She screams," hey, who stepped on my Starbucks cup? I was going to get a refill back on campus."

"You would think the king would be up there with Nipper," Choker says, acting like he wasn't scared from the dog bark or from crushing her cup.

"You mean the Wizard," Cresty says.

"The king should be here. The Nipper building is Utopia," Choker says, still trying to shake off being perfectly punked.

Turning out of the Nipper parking lot onto Front, the homeless looking man is pushing the empty shopping cart furiously with his head down and Abe Lincoln black stovepipe top hat pointed toward us. He speeds up more near us on the corner and yells, "Utopia? You mean dystopia, that's what you should mean," as he brushes shoulders with both Cresty and Choker, splitting us and continuing pushing toward City Hall and then looking back, allowing us to see our reflection off his mirror sunglasses.

"But this place isn't imaginary," Cresty yells. "Who are you? What do you want?"

The zombie hitchhiker with the Yankees hat on sideways follows him. He soon climbs into the shopping cart.

"Are you Booth's Avengers?" the hitchhiker yells.

We walk over yellow underground gas line markings - "G12" - on the red bricks of Market Street, past the parking lot booth with the guard still doing intermittent pushups inside and back toward the blue dumpster when Cliff texts: O-O N7c6.

"How many pushups today?" Choker asks.

"Never count," the guard says.

"How 'bout, what does the G12 yellow markings mean on the red bricks?" Cresty asks.

"G12?"

"Ya," she says pointing to the markings.

"Na. It is 219," the guard says. "You've been looking at it upside down and backwards."

Choker and Cresty both hop to the other side of the markings.

"If you say so," Choker says.

"How 'bout, then what does the 219 yellow

THE CHESS GAME

markings mean on the red bricks?" Cresty asks.

"By my count, I say its from Timothy 2:19."

"Timothy?" Choker and Cresty ask at once.

The guard recites: "The Lord knows those who are his and Everyone who confesses the name of the Lord must turn away from wickedness."

Cliff calls.

"Did you ever hear of Timothy, the one in the bible? Who is winning the chess game?" Cresty asks. "I can't follow the moves."

"You mean the Game of Chess," Ruby says, laughing into the speakerphone. "Not even Ruby himself can follow the moves."

"It's like life," Cliff says. "Just like in ancient China, the people couldn't follow the move of the dynasties and how when the USS Indy sunk, not making any moves sent waves of shock that shook the Navy.

"Paralyzed, the Navy took two weeks before making an official announcement. A half of month before a statement was made. The Navy hoped the news of the USS Indy sinking would be drowned by the announcement from President Truman… that Japan surrendered."

Sitting on top of the dumpster, legs swinging, Choker turns on his phone, slides the screen onto the music and sings U2's Until the End of the

KEVIN CALLAHAN

World:

>Haven't seen you in *such a pile*
>I was down the hold just *pissing* time
>Last time *life made sense* was *in Pete's* room
>We were as close together as a bride and groom
>We ate the food, we drank the wine
>Everybody having a good time
>Except *Pete*
>*Pete was* talking about the end of the world

Choker stands on one leg and walks like a tight-roper on the top of the dumpster. He stumbles a bit as he sings:

>*Pete* took *no* money
>*He* spiked *our* drink
>*We* miss *him* much these days *when we* stop to think

Choker flips open the lid of the dumpster with one leg and hums:

>*mmm mmmm mm mm* with those innocent eyes

THE CHESS GAME

>*mmm mmmm m mmmm* the element of surprise
>*mm mmm mmmmm* I was *ripping a mmm m mmmmmm mmmm mmmm* and broke *mmmm* heart
>*Pete was* talking about the end of the world

With stiff straight legs, he tap dances on the rim of the dumpster and sings in a deep voice:

> Love, love, love
> Love
> Love, love
> Love, love, love
> Love
> Love, love

"The song isn't about love," Cresty protests, snatching Choker's clenched hand as he hops down from the narrow dumpster dance floor. "Unless you consider it is a love song from Judas for Jesus."

"How?"

"The song is filled with scenes from "The Passion of the Christ." she says.

Choker continues singing passionately, making up words and searching for others:

In my dream *Pete* was drowning *his* sorrows
But *Pete's* sorrows, they learned to swim
Surrounding *Pete,* going down on *him*
Spilling over the brim
Waves of regret and waves of joy
I reached out for the one I *thought* to destroy
Pete, you'd said you'd wait
'Til the end of the world

    Outside the guarded L3 Building across from the Victor, an important looking man smokes – no he is vaping. A car alarm beeps incessantly inside the fenced L3 lot near two empty white patrol utility vehicles with the blue letters: SECURITY. Around the corner, only a few feet away, cigarette smoke waifs from where a group of more important looking men, and a woman, take their lunch break. They flip their butts into a concrete flowerpot filled with dead flowers and burnt bottle caps.
    "What does L3 mean?" Choker asks the vaper.
    "Ya. Are you all like spine researchers?" Cresty asks, reaching and pointing to the back of Choker's neck. "Which one is the L3 vertebrae?"
    "Don't know," the man says after a brief vape. "We're engineers. Not medical researchers."
    "Oh, sorry bro," Cresty says.
    "Sorry. No need to be," the vaping man says.

THE CHESS GAME

"Never thought how L3 could be the spine... interesting, like this company is the spine of the city and all the rebuilding is around the L3 here."

"Ya," says Cresty.

"Sorry," the vaping man says.

"Na. The vapors don't bother us," Cresty says rubbing me.

"Sorry... ahhh," he says again. "ahhh... I know one of the L's stand for Lockheed, which began as Martin Marietta but merged to become Lockheed Martin... the two other L's are companies, too, businesses which are part of L3 Communications."

"Sorry."

"Sir, don't be sorry, the info you told us is interesting," Choker says.

"No. Sorry," the vaping engineer tells us. "I can't even enjoy a real smoke... I'm working on the next generation atom bomb." He points to the clock on the City Hall tower, which says its 1:11.

"I should play that number," he says taking a puff on the shiny silver vape.

"But," Cresty says, "The clock is an hour behind."

THE CHESS GAME

Chapter 9

Choker spins while looking above him at City Hall, saying "we could be them for one day, but we should light out to the other side of Camden." Instead we make a left on Third Street and then a left on Cooper. We are on the edge of Rutgers' campus again. But we don't turn around. We light out toward the river, to the glow of the shining green skyscrapers of Philadelphia, down to the yellow mud on Front Street carried by the tires of construction vehicles from the suburbs.

We just made a loop.

Cresty and Choker must realize this orbit when we walk past the front of the "Parthenon looking" building, which is the first library we saw - but we approached earlier from the back. Now we've made a circle. Or are we behind the bank, the one near the prison?

"Huh. How?" Cresty says confused.

"What? So, the engineer is making the next generation atom bomb between casual vapes," Choker offers with surprising nonchalance. "Will… so Camden will build the next generation USS Indy to deliver the death? The circle of life… like our footsteps here."

"Maybe, for the job, the city will refurbish the

Battleship New Jersey ... "Cresty says.

A jogger sprints from across the street to the statue in front of the grand building. He is wearing a black ski cap, black tight fitting running pants, and a matching top that makes him look like a sleek scuba diver. He stretches his spine, twisting from side to side while weaving through the six columns of the library.

"It looks, this classical constructed monument of a building, worthy of being the National Library," Cresty says admiringly while glancing up and down over the mighty columns.

"But it must be... the Rutgers Camden Library," Choker says pausing... before cuing up his phone and then he starts singing U2's Ultra Violet Light My Way:

> Sometimes I feel like I *can't sow*
> Sometimes I feel like checkin' out
> I want to get it wrong
> Can't always be strong
> And love it won't last long...

The jogger stops stretching and twisting. He does a little dance to Choker's singing.

> Oh sugar, don't you cry

THE CHESS GAME

Oh child, wipe the tears from your eyes
You know I need you to be strong
And the day is as dark as the night is *wrong*
Feel like trash, you make me feel clean
I'm *a bit* black, can't see or be seen
Cresty, Cresty, Cresty... light my way
alright now
Cresty, Cresty, Cresty... light my way

Cresty rolls her head in rhythm of the song before she interrupts Bono's imposter and reads from her phone:

"The building here is part of Rutgers-Camden, you genius you, this Cooper Library in Johnson Park," she says, shoving Choker, who reaches out to her while feigning to fall away. "It was one of 36 Carnegie Libraries built here in New Jersey by Andrew Carnegie himself."

"You are... we're standing on a National Register of Historic Places place," the jogger says.

"How do you get to Carnegie Hall?" Choker asks the jogger.

"I know, practice, practice, practice," the jogger huffs in a tired tone.

"Nope... money, money, money," Choker responds.

From the middle of the street, either a college-age, no a high school-aged looking jaywalker wearing baggy clothes is pushing a skateboard. He zigzags up to us saying, "There is a mosaic in the entry named 'America Receiving the Gifts of Nations.' Which doesn't make sense. Does it? America is the one that gives. Like this library is a gift to the city. Doesn't make sense... like squatting in this city."

Looking as if he doesn't want to talk to us any more, he pushes his skateboard away from us wayward wanderers. Choker continues singing Ultra Violet Light My Way:

> You bury *our* treasure
> Where it can't be found
> But *our* love is like a secret
> That's been passed around
> There is a silence that comes to a house
> Where no one can sleep
> I guess it's the price of love
> I know it's not cheap
> *Cresty, Cresty, Cresty...* light my way
> oh, *be born*

While carrying his skateboard, the jaywalker zigzags back across Front Street, stopping in the

THE CHESS GAME

middle to sing: out "Light my way, squatters."

"At least you have a *ways*," Choker yells to him. "Nothing more can make me happy… happier in life except finding the toy king before leaving today."

"You mean the Wizard," Cresty says.

"You mean," the zigzagging jaywalker inquires, "you're not squatters moving in… squatting?"

So, we beat on, unknowingly to the stroke of a single skuller from Rutgers paddling under the Ben Franklin Bridge. Our steps match each pull. Where to now… we will walk around to find something that makes him, Choker, happy? I guess we will. There is another whole half of the downtown to search.

"You know what makes me laugh? Makes me happy? Happier?" Choker asks repetitively as if he won't wait for an answer.

"I know," Cresty says with certainty. "Telling old Pete stories, like the monk parable."

"Knowing why we are here," he says. "Why are we here?"

"Here in Camden? Here at the Parthenon-looking building?" Cresty asks, "Or… or here?"

There is a college-age looking loafer, with a droopy shoulder that sags in his 'Che Vive' t-shirt, leaning against the statue in front of the library.

Choker nudges him and says like an authoritarian, "You should be inside the library studying. Not lounging out here."

"Why are you here?" the loafer asks, not offended by the nudge.

"Here?" Cresty asks. "Here in Camden or… or here?"

"Looking for the… don't know," Choker responds. "Looking…"

"I'm looking, hoping a girl comes out of the library who saw me in there reading about shoulder surgery on the computer, hoping she picks me up and drives me back to Cherry Hill," the lopsided loafer says with his droopy shoulder drooping.

"You need an operation?" Cresty asks sympathetically. She suddenly thinks how fortunate she is to have two powerful shoulders from all those years of doing fingertip pushups, pushing as Pete counted.

"Sorry."

"Well, the doctor at Cooper Hospital just told me I need my right shoulder replaced," the worried loafer says. "He told me that he would use a reverse joint, that the ball wouldn't be connected to the top of the arm like standard surgeries, but would be attached to the shoulder."

"The doc would just be doing the procedure

THE CHESS GAME

backwards," Choker says with a glance of reassurance.

"That's all," Cresty adds, with a motherly rub on his slumped shoulder.

"And... this way... with the revolutionary surgery... your arm would be in your back," Choker quips. "You will be cool. You will have one arm in front and one arm in back. You will be able to wipe your butt easier... bro."

He ties to straighten his shoulder, but the 'Che Vive' t-shirt sags more.

"And you will be so interesting with windmill arms you will be able to pick up that girl in the library you are waiting for now," Choker says. "You won't need any pickup lines bro, you will have those crazy cool arms."

"I'd rather be crazy smart," he says.

"I know what you mean, Cresty's dad, Pete, told us how... about a decade ago... he was in the Black Rose late one night, many hours after the Lids had passed out from a day of drinking in Boston, when a college professor type, a lady around his age in her early 40's, sat at the empty stool between him and this 'intensely sick smart graduate school looking fine fellow,'" Choker rattles. "Pete said he was 'looking like his banged-up himself after a 12-hour bender' when the smart lady said to them both that she would go home with the guy who could use the word Timbuctoo in a four-line iambic pentameter poem.

"Pete said he drum-rolled his hands on the bar while saying da DUM, da DUM, da DUM, da DUM, da DUM.

"The real smart looking and young, mid-20-something guy, said he was in the master's program for Shakespearian Sonnets, specializing in free verse, at Harvard and told the lady "my pad or yours."

"Pete told the lady he was in the divinity program for Sea Isle Sinners when the other guy started:

> *Across the desert searing sand*
> *Moved a faceless caravan*
> *Man and camel, two by two*
> *Destination Timbuctoo*

"Pete said he downed his beer, grabbed the lady's hand, knelt down in front of her and said:

> *Me and Tim needed a rub*
> *Found three lasses in a pub*
> *They were three, we were two*
> *I bucked one, Tim bucked two*

THE CHESS GAME

"Pete said the lady stood up, pulled him to his feet... and they left the Black Rose Pub arm in arm 'and thought in thought.'"

Holding up the elbow of his bad shoulder, the loafer floats back into the library. He stops at the front door between two majestic columns and lifts his right arm skyward, as if he can clean the top of the columns with what he said was his bad shoulder. He waves with a laugh, making the 'Che Vive' t-shirt flutter.

"Che' and me, Vive El Che'," Choker pants in iambic pentameter.

We wander up toward the City Hall tower, which says its 2:22... but is an hour behind.

We follow the River LINE up Cooper Street. A Rutgers Business School advertisement splashes the entire side of the River LINE rattling toward us.

We stand rigid in front of the United States Courthouse on Fourth and Cooper Streets. The front steps are flanked with ramps angling up each side. With his back to us, the homeless looking man is pushing the shopping cart up the ramp. The hitchhiker wearing the Yankees hat on sideways and holding his lace-less sneakers is seated, scrunched in the cart. With his Able Lincoln hatted titled sideways, he pushes down the ramp, pulling on the cart near the bottom so the passenger he is carrying doesn't roll away. He turns around and pushes up the ramp again allowing us to see ourselves in his mirror sunglasses. He does this a few times before we walk south on Fourth Street, back to where we were an hour or so ago even though the clock on City Hall says it was two hours or so ago...

In the middle of the block, we can see how the courthouse is actually a separate building behind the post office. The buildings are connected by a second-floor walkway and guarded by a man in an official looking red beret sitting in a booth with a metal red roof. There is a metal gate that rises from the ground that blocks the front of the driveway between the two important buildings.

A man wearing an all white suit, a black tie and white shoes is sliding out of a white Cadillac Escalade. The man in the funny red lid leaves his booth to stop the first man from putting a quarter into the parking meter.

"I need to pick up a certified mail receipt," the man in the white suit says.

"Just go into the post office," the booth man says.

"No. I need to pick up the receipt from the courthouse."

The man in the red beret says, "Just go into the

THE CHESS GAME

courthouse... I will guard your car from *Big Bro*... looking down on you, us like a tight-roper in the sky."

"Thank you."

"Yo-Yo will protect your wheels," the booth man says.

The spiffy suit and tie man comes out after a few minutes. He holds a receipt, waves it with satisfaction and gratitude. Yo-Yo sticks out his hand.

The man opens the door of his Cadillac as he reaches into his pocket and hands Yo-Yo a dollar bill.

Yo-Yo keeps his hand out. The man hands him another dollar as he slides into his low-riding Cadillac.

Choker reaches into his pants, his back pocket. He pulls out his buzzing phone. Cliff sent another text: Be3 d6

Cresty stares down the man extorting parking payments as Yo-Yo reaches out to stick one of the dollar bills in the back pocket of the meter maid lady dressed in a tight-fitting blue uniform and holding the hand of a young girl. The dollar bill just floats to the ground.

Acting like she doesn't see Yo-Yo's move, Cresty pulls out the pamphlet from her pocket.

"In 1977, Romero's Jesuit priest friend was working with the poor, building self reliance groups for them," Cresty says as Yo-Yo lounges back into the booth, sliding down his red beret over his eyes while leaning back in his chair. He tells us he has a night job so he needs his shut-eye.

"His friend was assassinated," Cresty continues as Choker studies the meter maid and the young girl walking toward Rutgers. "Romero pleaded with the government to investigate the murder... but the G-men didn't."

Cliff sends another text:

> MY DAD STARTED PLAYING CHESS BY HIMSELF ON THE OVERTURNED RAFT WHEN ANGEL FLOPPED BACK ON THE RAFT ... ASKED TO PLAY AGAIN... MY DAD OPENED WITH THE SAME KING PAWN FORWARD TWO SPACES TO E4 ... THE ATLANTIC CITY MAN AGAIN FOLLOWED WITH HIS BISHOP PAWN TWO SPACES TO F5 ... THE UNCOLORED MAN WITH SLICKED HAIR LAUGHED AGAIN SAYIING "NOT THIS TIME SAILOR."

Uncaring and flippant, Cresty approaches the booth and reads to Yo-Yo through the glass door:

THE CHESS GAME

"Later, in 1979, the Revolutionaries took power of the government after the Salvadoran Civil War. Romero pleaded with the U.S. government not to give military aid to the new Junta, stating it would only increase the injustice and repression, but..."

An amused Yo-Yo opens the door of the booth and approaches a Land Rover pulling into the empty space as Cresty reads:

"... but President Jimmy Carter ignored Romero's begging."

The street show beats on as Choker continues singing Ultra Violet Light My Way:

> Baby, baby, baby... light my way
> Oh ... ultraviolet...
> Ultraviolet ...
> Ultraviolet ...
> *Ultrasound ...*
> Baby, baby, baby... light my way

We wander away from the booth and the entertained guard. Cresty looks back and sees Yo-Yo poke his hand in the window of the Land Rover. Choker keeps singing:

> I remember
> When we *heard the Rolling Stones*

Now we lie together
In whispers and moans
When I was all messed up
And I had *basketball* in my head
Your love was a light bulb
Hanging over my bed
Cresty, Cresty, Cresty ... light my way
oh, come on
Baby, baby, baby... light *our ways*
Supersonic ...

"You know," Cresty says to Choker, "the song is all about the cruelty of God's reticence… where is He at? How come He isn't looking down on you, us like a tight-roper in the sky."

"You mean Her," Choker says smiling.

She sings:

We bury *our* treasure where it can't be found,
But *our* love is like a secret that's been passed around.
There is a silence that comes to a house
Where no one *says peep.*
I guess it's the price of love; I know it's not cheap.

THE CHESS GAME

"You know in the chorus, Bono alludes to the Book of Job that is what '*baby, baby, baby, light my way*' is about, what it is referring to," Cresty says, "while ultraviolet love is a clever metaphor for God being invisible in our little lives, while doing our daily duties, walking around the streets of Camden... singing... searching... not squatting... looking for the Wizard."

"You mean the king," Choker says before singing:

> Baby, baby, baby ...
> Baby, baby, baby ...
> Baby, baby, baby ... light my way

Rubbing her belly – me, Cresty adds:

> Baby, baby, baby... light *our* way ... *ways!*

"*Ways?*" Choker asks as the Land Rover drives by us. "*The* king is not over here... not in the loafer's hair... not in the booth there... let's go to the other side of Camden."

At the corner of Fourth and Market, where the law office building stands, we see a flock of birds munching on the pile of birdseed. The small birds suddenly twirl and fly right toward us and over a lady dressed nicely all in black using an umbrella as a cane. The young-looking jaywalker in baggy clothes stops zigzagging, flies his skateboard over the curb and into the street, and yells at her, "They almost took you out... they, the birds, almost took you out." But the lady just keeps walking as if she never saw the birds.

Further down Fourth Street, past where the River LINE curves, the jogger who is dressed like a scuba diver stops in front of us on the street. Out of breath, he slumps against the gas pump behind the Fire Administration building on the corner of Arch Street.

"I should play that number," the resting jogger says, pulling on the sleeves of his tight outfit.

"Yup ... but it is an hour behind," Choker says, nodding to the tardy tower clock.

"No, no, no... the number seven," he says pulling on Choker's shirt. "Did you know Jesus performed seven miracles on the Sabbath?"

"It's not the Sabbath today," Choker says. "Is it?"

THE CHESS GAME

Chapter 10

We are now officially wandering the streets. I use wander instead of walk, for a reason because that's what this walk feels like. But really, we are *wandering* now more than before. Are we looking for the king? The Wizard? Or Choker's forsaken felicity? I know, I'm throwing around big words like simple thoughts, but I'm hoping to make a favorable impression since I know nothing about life yet and to reinsure you the confusion in these streets is in my head, too. And, as if a tribute to myself for continuing on, imploring you to do the same, knowing already the path to truth, to justice for all, is a long one.

As the temperature suddenly dips, a mysterious mist drifts in from the Delaware River. We can't see Philly across the water anymore. We can hear each oar gently splash into the river water, though, from the single skuller below the bridge.

Mist? Midday? In June?

As if on cue, the River LINE's wheels squeak like a foghorn as we look up to the City Hall clock. Our beacon. We can barely see the top of the tower for the guidance we need.

Out of the mist, the homeless looking man pushing the empty shopping card stands on the platform of the River LINE at the new Walter Rand Transportation Center.

"You are at Nirn," the homeless looking man bellows from the other side of the tracks while removing his mirror sunglasses.

He is looking at us, but the mist hides his face. He steps to the edge of the platform and says, "Here at Martin Luther King Boulevard and Broadway you can catch the PATCO Speedline to Philly and New Jersey Transit buses to New York... or Greyhound buses to... I guess, anywhere."

"Nirvana?" Choker asks.

"No, Nirn," says a man from our side of the tracks. He is holding a basket of fruit with one hand and scrolling down the screen of his handheld video game with the other,

"He's talking about the hub, the wheel, the center of Mundus," the multi-tasking man adds. "You don't know about the heavens yet... I guess."

Choker jumps on the tracks to cross, but an oncoming train's wheels squeaks like a foghorn, a warning and bouncing him back onto the platform.

"Catch Me If You Can," says the homeless looking man in the L. L. Bean vest and with his mirror sunglasses back on as the mist rises.

"What for?" Choker asks, pacing on the

THE CHESS GAME

platform, edging to the yellow line as the train passes.

"To find the Wizard," the **man holding the basket of fruit and scrolling down the screen of his handheld video game** says.

"How?"

"As the parable goes, two wee little brown mice fell in a bucket of milky cream," the man says, putting down the fruit and video game on the platform and making hand gestures, like a swimming motion. "The first mouse quickly buckled and drowned. The second mouse refused to quit. He **grinded** so hard that eventually he **churned** the cream into butter …

"And danced out of the bucket."

Choker jumps on the tracks to try and cross again, but another train's wheels squeaks like a foghorn from the other direction. Again, he bounces back on the platform.

When the train passes, the Abe Lincoln hat man is gone… but the cardboard sign "The Wizard will fix everything" leans up against a pole.

So is the mist… gone.

Choker crosses the tracks and picks up the cardboard sign. He walks up to the crosswalk and waits for us.

"The River LINE runs up the middle of Martin

Luther King," Choker says as he turns suddenly toward Cresty.

"King? You would think the king would be on a street named Martin Luther King," Choker proclaims diplomatically.

"You mean the Wizard," Cresty says, touching the sign under his arm.

A teenage girl wearing a catholic high school uniform, a white top and a plaid green skirt, walks while trying to cover a hole in her black stocking with her hand. The hole is near the bottom of the hem of her dress, which is high on her thigh, so her hand barely reaches. Scraping her shoes, she hustles past us as our eyes explore up and down Martin Luther King Boulevard.

"Which way is PATCO?" the girl stops and asks us from behind. "I don't know my ways around here. Balls. I'm late for school. Really late."

"Across from city hall," Cresty says, pointing up to the tower clock off to our right. "It's good you are finding your *ways.*

"Ways, ma'am," she says, "is all Jesus gives you."

She looks up to the City Hall clock and says, "Thank you Mary, Joe and Jesus. It's only 11:33. I thought it was later. I can make school by noon."

A mini blue dump truck pulls a utility trailer

THE CHESS GAME

with the company name: SOLUTIONS. The truck turns the corner onto MLK, forcing us to take a step back onto the curb. The heavy trailer and the overstressed hitch of the truck scrape the road.

The scraping sounds sends chills through us. We decide to turn toward the porch, go back just as Cliff calls on the cell.

"Evidence was withheld from the people," he whispers on the speakerphone. "Not until a court martial hearing for the USS Indy, for Captain McVay was vital information finally released to the public. It was ... the inquiry determined... that the Navy sent McVay into 'harm's way' and denied his request for an escort by a destroyer.

"He assumed the waters were safe. Still he zigzagged the Indy just to be safe... safer."

"We're on our ways to the safety of the porch," Cresty declares into the speakerphone.

"You mean the Porch of Versailles," Ruby laughs into the phone. "Stop to see the gardens ..."

Another hint? Cresty wonders as Choker says, "Ruby could be feeding us misinformation ... to keep us off the trail ... like the Navy did."

A black and white Camden County cop car idles on the corner with its lights flashing, stopping traffic for a pregnant woman in a short black skirt and high heels. She is walking purposely across the street holding an empty lemon Gatorade bottle. She stops at the corner. The man wearing the all white suit and black tie behind her opens the door to his Cadillac Escalade. The lady keeps walking. He turns into the street level parking lot of the Rand Center.

Across the street we can see the original Ronald McDonald House where families can stay for free when their kids are being treated for cancer at Cooper Hospital. A family of four stands in front of the statue of the family of four. The mother is wearing a shroud, covering her face.

Cliff sends a text:

> AFTER MY DAD OPENED WITH THE SAME KING PAWN FORWARD TWO SPACES TO E4 AND THE ATLANTIC CITY MAN WITH FOLLOWED WITH HIS SAME BISHOP PAWN TWO SPACES TO F5 MY DAD ATTACKED WITH HIS ADVANCED PAWN ON THE DIAGONAL E4XF5 TO CAPTURE THE UNCOLORED MAN WITH SLICKED HAIR ADVANCE PAWN ... ANGEL TOOK THE BAIT AGAIN AND MOVED HIS KNIGHT PAWN FORWARD TWO SPACES TO G5 ...

We wander past a variety of stores with broken

THE CHESS GAME

lights on Broadway, including the crowded Rainbow Clothes shop and Goldwaite Jewelers, which sells rose-colored wigs. The two stores sandwich an empty building displaying a red block-lettered sign. The sign looks as if it once read "Maximum Tax Returns," but some added red graffiti makes it look like ... "Marxism Max Reruns."

A teenage kid in a rainbow-colored hoodie and tan-yellow construction boots cuts across Broadway, cutting off a shirtless guy crossing Broadway going the other way. His shoes have no laces and he is carrying a black and white jacket and a red backpack.

Cliff texts the next two chess move against Ruby: Nc3 Qg6. Choker doesn't let her see the moves, as if he knows what the moves mean.

We turn back and walk, well, wander down MLK Boulevard toward the river.

Cresty wonders why we aren't going toward the porch. Was there a clue in the chess moves?

On the right we pass a CVS Drug store commanding a full corner. It is on the same side of the street as the train depot, but we are on the other side of MLK. The pregnant lady with the short skirt walks out from the parking garage holding an empty lemon Gatorade bottle. She sits on the lime green fire hydrant across from a yellowish-brown brick building, with slots for windows.

The shirtless guy without laces to secure his flappy black shoes knocks on the door of the prison. After banging for a few minutes with no answer, he approaches us. He sits on his black and white jacket and leans up against his backpack.

"What you *is* reading?" he asks Cresty, who is sitting on the cardboard sign with her feet hanging over the curb.

"Unlike the Marxist calling, Romero followed the Catholic vision of Liberation Theology," Cresty says without looking up, reading out of the pamphlet. "He didn't believe in liberation with its foundation, its core belief rooted in violence."

The lady with the short skirt pops up and walks along the tracks on MLK and makes a right following the curve of the railroad. We walk down MLK Boulevard toward the river, to an oval with a gold propeller that welcomes you to the Camden Waterfront at the end of the street with a large lettered sign: MLK BOULEVARD.

Cresty continues reading to the shirtless man following us. "Oscar believed in the church of the poor, not in the church of the rich."

"He would be liking it here," the shirtless man says.

THE CHESS GAME

We look to the right and see that in front of the aquarium is the Camden Children's Garden

"The garden," Cresty says. "There it is. The garden Ruby told us about."

Choker is looking across the street at Vitarelli's on the Delaware Café and Bistro.

"Should we eat?" Choker asks. "Weren't you thirsty, Cresty?"

Cresty speed walks along the River LINE in the middle of the street. She stops in front of the Walt Whitman box office.

Choker and the shirtless man stay across the street.

"Old Walt is now selling tickets," the shirtless man says. "Ironic, huh? Walt wrote Leaves of Grass, using the pun grass, which was a term given by publisher to literary works of minor value and leaves, which were pages printed.

"He died here in Camden a hundred years before the city did. He is buried here under a mound of leaves."

"Where?" Choker asks, edging closer toward the shirtless man.

"Where the Streets Have No Name," the shirtless man says laughing and then hopping on the back of a River LINE car as it passes going north, joining the homeless looking man in the L. L

KEVIN CALLAHAN

Bean vest, wearing the Abe Lincoln black stovepipe top hat and mirror sunglasses. He pulls his rattling shopping cart behind him and then grabs his cardboard sign from Cresty.

Choker starts chasing the train when his phone rings. The unknown caller hangs up. Choker plays his phone. He sings:

> I wanna run, I want to hide
> *They* wanna tear down *city hall*
> That hold *them* inside.
> I wanna reach out
> And touch the flame
> Where the streets have no name.

The shirtless man jumps off the back of the train and walks along the tracks toward the Ben Franklin Bridge. He waves for us to follow. Choker continues singing:

> I wanna feel sunlight on my face
> I see the dust-cloud
> *Re-appear* with *each pace*
> I wanna take shelter
> From the poison *refrain*
> Where the streets have no name
> Where the streets have no name

THE CHESS GAME

Where *Camden* has no *more fame*

 We follow the shirtless man on the tracks toward the bridge and up to the Victor. We are making a circle again without going to the other side of downtown. Choker pauses his music and says to Cresty, "We're making a loop, like Loopy the jitney driver in Sea Isle."
 "Ya. But Loopy had a path," Cresty says.
He plays his phone and sings:

> We're still building and burning down love
> Burning down love.
> And when I go there
> I go there with you

Cresty interjects:

> It's all *we* can do

And Choker continues:

> This city's *amok*, and *its* love turns to rust
> Its beaten and blown by the wind
> Trampled in dust.
> I'll show you a place
> High *and without pain*

We make a sudden right and walk back up Market Street; back toward City Hall.

Choker sings:

> Wher*e Camden has* no *more fame*
> Where the streets have no name
> Where *Camden has* no *more shame*
> Where the streets have no name.
> We're still building and burning down love
> Burning down love
> And when *we* go there
> *We* go there with you

"That's all you... we can do, "Cresty sings, finishing the song.

She then says, "You know how Pete talked 'Stonesbaskosophy' in Sea Isle with Loopy and everyone else, mixing the Rolling Stones, basketball and philosophy, but he truly thought it was Bono who was a modern-day apostle of Jesus... not Mick and Keith.

"He told me when he saw U2 's second ever Philly show on December 1, 1984, how *his Irish lads* opened with Tick Tock, closed with the song 40... how he thought sitting in the second row of the balcony at the Tower Theater was the 'grandest night of his life'... and how he vowed, as the

THE CHESS GAME

Upper Darby building's bricks shook that night, how every night had to be the grandest of his life…

"This day, when we get back to the hospital, will be the grandest day of our lives."

The sudden and mysterious mist returns, dropping like being sprayed from a tight-roper above.

The teenage kid in the rainbow-colored hoodie and tan-yellow construction boots cuts in front of us on Broadway and Market Streets.

"Don't breathe," the kid says, pulling his rainbow hoodie over his face and covering his mouth.

"Why?" both Choker and Cresty ask.

"When the wind shifts and blows from the south, the smoke from the trash-to-steam plant near Sacred Heart Church blows up to the city."

Cresty covers her mouth and holds me with her other hand.

"The breeze will die, so don't worry," the teenage kid mumbles into his hoodie. "Then the fog disappears… and you can breathe again."

We watch the rainbow-colored hoodie fade into the mist and then vanish. He is out of our lives as swiftly as the mist over the river has lifted and the breeze from the river returns. Looking west down Market Street, we can see City Hall in

Philadelphia, making the two cities look connected.

"I say," Cresty repeats, "I say, this day, when we get back to the hospital … this day will be the grandest of our lives. Like Pete's U2 concert at the Tower Theater."

"This day, I say, will be," Choker adds seamlessly, "if we find the king.

"That is a fact."

"That," Cresty says, "is that."

THE CHESS GAME

Chapter 11

After Choker reminds us how we have to find the other side of the city, with blatant obsequiousness, (yeah, again, although I'm an unborn baby I can show off, too) Cresty hops on the River LINE and we ride back on the noisy, bumpy train toward the aquarium.

We step off the train outside of the BB&T theater complex. Under the overpass a street man is playing, or banging, on four upside-down plastic buckets with wooden drumsticks. There are four early-teenage girls line dancing behind him, sliding on outdoor tiles to the beat da DUM, da DUM, da DUM, da DUM, da DUM. The youngest girl is out of step, but she can't hide her frozen smile.

"If only there was a hotel in the city with dancing and music where we could all go," the man banging on the buckets says to us.

We wander, actually we head directly over to the red and white brick façade of the music pavilion's VIP club entrance. The gate is open. We go inside and walk right directly to the front of the concert stage. We sit on the edge of the stage and look out to the open sky above the grass, which spreads up a gentle hill toward the river behind the enclosed seating area. Cresty leans back with a tired sigh and then lays on the stage. Choker jumps up on the stage and in a mocking old English voice, he speaks into the live microphone: "All the world's a stage. And all the men and women merely players."

A man on a ladder near the back curtain who is working on the lighting overhead says: "They have their exits and their entrances."

Startled, Cresty hops up and shuffles on weary legs up the main aisle toward the open air. Choker follows, saying to the lighting man, "Shakespeare… All's Well That Ends Well."

"As You Like It," the lighting man says.

"I like it," Choker says, looking back to the man and giving him a hesitant, thumbs up. "I was an English major my freshman year in college at Ursinus before dropping out like J.D. Salinger."

"This is Walt Whitman's town, so," the lighting man says politely, "properly, you should be quoting *the* Walt and not t*he* Bard."

While walking backward, Choker tells the lighting man, "Right on. But Walt never equated the world to a stage,"

Flicking on the back overhead-lights, the man on the ladder says, "Read on."

"Nope. Tell me," Choker demands.

THE CHESS GAME

Standing on the top rung of the ladder, the man recites:

> They live in brothers, again ready to defy you;
> They were purified by death,
> They were taught and exalted.
> Not a grave of those slaughtered ones,
> But is growing its seed of freedom,
> In its turn to bear seed,
> Which the winds shall carry afar and resow,
> And the rain nourish.
> Not a disembodied spirit
> Can the weapon of tyrants let loose,
> But it shall stalk invisibly over the earth,
> Whispering, counseling, cautioning.
> Liberty, let others despair of thee,
> But I will never despair of thee:
> Is the house shut? Is the master away?
> Nevertheless, be ready, be not weary of watching,
> He will surely return; his messengers come anon.

The lightning man bows on the ladder. He returns to work, as Walt would like.

As he turns around, Choker sees a college-age

girl sitting in the end seat of one of the middle rows. She is holding a white towel. As Choker walks closer, he looks relieved and asks, "Cresty, what is in the towel?"

Hearing no answer, he nudges closer... and jumps back when he sees the face of the baby wrapped in the towel. The newborn baby is dead.

"Cresty," he screams. We hear him even though we are already walking out on the grass and up the hill.

"What?" Cresty yells back.

The lady holding the baby looks up. She looks exactly like Cresty. Red hair tied in ponytail. Even her shoulders are strong like her jaw.

"What t-t-t-the ... "Choker stutters. He sprints over to the grass area to where we are. He sees us and then looks back at the college-age girl, who is walking out the VIP entrance.

He chases the lady outside, but she is gone. Choker runs back inside. He is shaking, and he lies down next to us in the grass.

"Cresty," he says. "If you are here, well then, I just saw your Doppelganger."

But Cresty already is asleep on the hill.

THE CHESS GAME

In Cresty's dream, we cross the river from Camden to Philadelphia on a tightrope. Looking down, I see Penn Treaty State Park.

The wind whispers: "On this historic ground along the Delaware River is where William Penn met with native Americans in 1682 and, legend says, made a handshake deal under a large oak tree for friendship and goodwill. British troops, who had heard of the legend, guarded the tree during the Revolutionary War so it wouldn't be cut down for firewood… then, in 1910, the great tree where Penn and the Lenni-Lenapes met, fell.

We all sleep until we awaken when we hear a thud. The lighting ladder fell. Without missing a beat, though, we can hear the man with his four buckets tapping away on stage.

"Time for some backbeat music," he says, turning to the four dancers and pointing to the clock on the City Hall tower that we can see from the grassy hill here, which says it's 3 o'clock sharp… but it is an hour behind.

Turning on his phone, Choker sings U2's Gloria. The man keeps beat with the buckets. Cresty falls back to sleep as Choker's voice cracks:

    I *cry* to sing this song
    I, I try to stand up

KEVIN CALLAHAN

But I *don't mind this feat*
I *cry*, I try to speak up
But only in you I'm complete
Gloria in te domine
Gloria exultate
Gloria, Gloria

  Cliff texts his chess moves: Kh1 Bg4… Choker keeps singing. The man keeps beating, keeping beat with the buckets.

Oh Lord, loosen my lips
I *cry* to sing this song
I, I *cry* to get in
But I can't find the door
The door is open
You're standing there
You let me in
Gloria in te domine
Gloria exultate
Oh Lord, if I *knew* anything
Anything *I saw*
I'd give *all* to you
I'd give *the ball* to you

THE CHESS GAME

Carrying his buckets toward us, the drumming man says, "You two, I love the Christianity of U2, too."

He turns the four buckets over and says, "Why don't we all sit down, the four of us."

"What do you mean?" Choker asks.

"Gloria has a liturgical chorus, sung in Latin," the drummer says. "Liturgical like your Number seven jersey. Jesus told seven parables in the gospel of Matthew 13. Maybe I should play 13."

"Did you see a young lady walk out of here carrying a baby wrapped in a white towel?" Choker asks him.

"Gloria," he says.

"Is that her name?" Choker asks.

"Keep singing Gloria," he says, tapping away on his buckets.

"Can't."

"Glory! I just had a dream about Oscar Romero giving glory to God," Cresty says, waking up.

"In the dream, I was looking down on a giant oak tree which stood on the banks of the Delaware River in Philadelphia ... birds took the acorns from the tree across the river and buried them in Camden ... oak trees sprouted on the Camden side ... but the other trees in Camden, the established ones with roots, though, told the oak saplings they couldn't stay on this side of the river ... the baby trees had to uproot themselves and swim across the river ... some trees never made it across, back home ... the others that did never were replanted ... they died on the roots of the giant oak tree at Penn Treaty Park."

The bucket man beats da DUM, da DUM, da DUM, da DUM, da DUM. Cresty continues:

"The giant oak tree, with the human face of Oscar Romero said to the dying saplings, 'Moses never reached the Promise Land, David never built The Temple and John the Baptist never left the King's dungeon with his head... but when they met God, they all heard the words, 'Well done my good and faithful servants.' "

"Why wasn't Oscar Romero in your dream?" Choker asks.

"He was the oak tree. Weren't you listening?" Cresty scolds him. She continues to speak of Romero's Spiritual life.

"Oscar gave glory to God by desiring to be holy. He wondered how far a soul can rise if a person lets himself be possessed fully by God," she says. "Like Bono sings with the words Gloria exultate."

The bucket man says The BB&T Pavilion was "supposed to bring glory to the city."

THE CHESS GAME

"It opened as the Tweeter Center in 1995 and then changed its name to The Susquehanna Bank Center," the man says. "But this 25,000-seat open-air amphitheater has never been able to change the fortunes of Camden even though the seats fill up.

"Suburban kids drink in the parking lots before the shows because there aren't any bars besides the Victor. The kids go home after the shows to drink, too ... but on their way home they stop to buy drugs ... then they eventually end up in the jail ...

"If only ... if only they built hotels in the city with dancing and music ...

"Instead, the Camden Children's Garden opened on the Waterfront. It is filled with imaginary exhibits, like Storybook Gardens, the Dinosaur Gardens, and the Giant Picnic Gardens.

"And, oh yeah, the kid's play garden has a Tree House. Who lives in a Tree House? A city can't be rebuilt with tree houses. A city needs hotels with dancing and music."

The bucket man beats da DUM, da DUM, da DUM, da DUM, da DUM.

Cliff texts:

> AGAIN MY DAD MOVED HIS QUEEN ON THE DIAGONAL TO H5 AND HAD THE ATLANTIC CITY MAN IN CHECK MATE IN THREE

Moves ... the uncolored man with slicked hair should've learned and moved his pawn forward two paces to block the queen ... Instead he moved into checkmate again ... In disgust he flipped over the raft ... The coral pieces floated... My dad collected the pieces and board and tried to climb back on the capsized raft ... But this time the raft was ripped... and sunk ...

We follow the bucket man and walk down the center aisle. Choker stops and looks at the seat the lady was sitting in, the one who he saw that looked exactly like Cresty. A white towel is draped over the armrest. There is no dead baby.

"Let's get out of here. You would *not* think the king would be at an amphitheater that keep changes names," Choker says.

"You mean the Wizard," Cresty says.

"I guess we lost the homeless looking man in the L.L. Bean vest," Choker says, sounding relieved. "I guess he found the guy in the Yankees hat to put in his shopping cart and doesn't want to push it anymore.

"Or," Choker continues, "He might have found

his *ways*."

"Or more w*ays*," Cresty says. "Did you ever get a good look at his face?"

"Nope. His face? I'm always looking at his hands when he gets close, making sure he doesn't stab or shoot us. Why?"

"He looks just like you."

"What?"

"Doppelganger. Do you know what that is?" she asks.

"Yup. A look-alike, or body double," Choker says. "Some think it is a paranormal phenomenon while others think it is time travel, like a picture of a civil war soldier who looks like a modern Hollywood actor."

"Yeah, well, without the mirror sunglasses, through the mist, even with the Abe Lincoln black stovepipe top hat, the shopping cart guy looks just like you, light skin with the same part in your hair. Freaky."

"Yeah, especially since I just saw your… since a Doppelganger is usually a harbinger for misfortune."

We walk out the exit door of the VIP entrance while the bucket man taps away on stage again and the four girls dance behind him.

The lighting man picks up the ladder and says,

"Good without evil is like light without darkness… which in turn is like righteousness without hope."

"I will read Walt," Choker tells him.

"It's Shakespeare," the lighting man says. "I just recited *the* Bard and not *the* Walt."

"Of course," Choker says, "Yup. As You Like It."

Turning off the backlight above, he says, "No. All's Well That Ends Well."

A train chugs past us outside of the BB&T theater complex as Cresty asks, "What was that about?"

"Just talking Shakespeare."

"Oh, you mean how," Cresty says looking up at the clock tower, "fair is foul, and foul is fair."

"Macbeth," Choker says clapping his hands, also looking up at the clock tower, "from the three witches of Macbeth… when stirring the cauldron."

THE CHESS GAME

Chapter 12

Across Federal Street from Cooper Hospital, the PATCO Hi-Speedline coming in, zooming from the South Jersey suburbs, dips underground and below Broadway.

A refreshing light breeze stirs as we wait for the traffic light to change. The two men in yellow jackets, with the slogan KEEPING CAMDEN CLEAN AND SAFE on the bottom of their back in black letters, are behind us. But they aren't pushing yellow trashcans on wheels. The one with the name Caesar stitched on his jacket's front chest pocket tells us that he is a "Citizen from Tent City under the 676 overpass." The other man just keeps walking – right through the red traffic light.

"When the wind blows, even a *bit*, the traffic lights go out," Caesar explains. "You will wait all day at this light... almost as torturous as waiting *bit by bit* for George Washington's tent to come..."

"I thought when the wind blows a bit, well the smog from the South Camden trash burning facility covers the city," Choker says.

"When the wind blows from the south," Caesar says. "When the wind blows from the west, from across the river, from the Philly side with the

William Penn and Rocky statues, the traffic lights stop."

"All of them?"

"Some of them."

Caesar then berates Choker and Cresty, "The homeless tents are moving now to the Cathedral, not even waiting for George Washington's tent to come here, moving outside the rectory and on the pedestrian street. I'm just a worker. Before this job, I sandblasted the cathedral.

"Now, the government wants to shut us down," the man adds. "I'm working but don't make enough money even to live in the row homes in this city. Where will we live? We have nowhere to go."

"You can follow us," Choker says. "Like the guy with the shopping cart and mirror sunglasses has been doing all day."

Caesar walks through the red traffic light. Cars follow him. The intersection is blocked with vehicles going both ways. We zigzag between the stuck cars.

He turns to us from the other side of the street and with his hand out and palm open, he says, "Render to Caesar what is Caesar's and render to God what is God's."

We pass Cooper Hospital. We still have over four hours until the doc takes my picture. We don't

THE CHESS GAME

make a right down Benson Street to the porch. Instead Choker sprints straight ahead. In front of us are two lanes of cobblestone on Seventh Street. There is an inviting boulevard of grass in the middle of the lanes. There are benches and a gravel walkway in the middle of the grass boulevard.

Behind us, the shopping cart rattles. The empty cart is being pushed over the cobblestones. The rattling stops when we sit on a bench under one of the Cooper Hospital flags. The expensive flags are red with gold letters. The banners look majestic hanging on the Kelly-green lampposts.

The man in the L.L Bean vest is looking down, his Abe Lincoln hat pointing at us, as he kicks at one of the loose cobblestones.

Ignoring him, Choker calls up on his phone the exact location of the Martin Luther King College House while Cresty reads the pamphlet on Romero's last day.

"On March 24 of 1980, Romero was celebrating Mass at a hospital chapel called 'La Divina Providencia," she says. "In his sermon, he urged Salvadoran soldiers to follow God's higher law and to cease continuing the government's repression of human rights.

"When he was done, Romero was shot dead."

The gray gravel we are walking on turns into

red bricks when the Cooper Hospital flags disappear behind us.

We make a left on Walnut Street to visit the MLK College House.

"You would think … if the king isn't on King Street, it has to be at the old Martin Luther King house," says Choker.

"Yeah, you would think the king had to be here."

"You mean the Wizard," Cresty says.

The MLK College House has no markers or signs to show, to prove that he once lived here. There is just a flagstone façade. No fancy flags like on the light posts outside Cooper Hospital.

The dented aluminum siding on the left side, next to an open lot, is painted gray. MLK's old house is number 753. It is on the left side of a duplex. The front door is boarded up.

Fumbling and then flipping his phone from the map of this checkered city to his music, Choker sings U2's Pride in the Name of Love:

> One man come in the *game* of love
> One man come and go
> One man come *free* to justify
> One man to overthrow
> In the name of love

THE CHESS GAME

Who more in the name of love
In the *blame* of love
What more in the *shame* of love
One man caught *without bit of sense*
One man he resist
One man washed *without any reach*
One man betrayed with a kiss
In the *shame* of love
What more in the *blame* of love
In the *fame* of love
What more in the *game* of love

Next to the house, in the grass lot, there are three old men playing baseball.

"Actually, we're playing *half*-ball," the outfielder says to us. "Throw *dem* strikes, my man, swing the bat, batter, it's blazin' hot out here and *dese* kids here are buggin' me."

"Half what?" Choker asks.

"It was an immensely popular version of baseball in the streets of Camden and Philadelphia in the 1930s to 1950s," he says, changing his voice from baseball banter to a TV announcer's tone.

"Back in our day, this was the big thing in the neighborhood," the pitcher yells to us."

"Very few of the kids could afford a pimple ball," the chubby batter says. "They were 5 cents."

"So, we would cut the balls in half," the man holding a bat, but serving as catcher, too, says. "*Hal*fball."

"Why did you cut the ball in half?" Cresty asks.

"To save money," the catcher says. "And to save windows," the pitcher says.

"We didn't want to break a window," the outfielder says, who comes closer toward us, near the boarded-up windows in the old MLK House. "Our parents would've *breaken* our butts."

"You see, you couldn't hit a halfball as hard," the pitcher says, "wouldn't break any windows... folks wouldn't break our butts."

"And you couldn't hit the ball as far," the batter says, "so less chance of losing the ball."

"And you got two balls for the price of one," Cresty says, while swinging an air bat like the on-deck batter.

"Why do you still play?" Choker questions. "No offense... but you guys probably can afford new balls. And, like I said, no offense, but there are no windows, really, to break around here, except the house a block over... and those windows are boarded up."

"Babe, once hit that house," the pitcher says, pointing to the pudgy left-handed batter. "He was just seven-years-old at the time."

THE CHESS GAME

"Yeah, it does make me feel young, still playing," the pitcher says. "And, it is our *ways* to stay together. We've been playing for 70-some years now.

"We played here when ships were built in Camden... we played here when Unruh went on... we played here when Nipper was taken down... we played here when the Camden 28 was let go... we played here when Nipper was put up... we played here when Camden will be again being...

"Always on this lot."

"The lot isn't that big, but cozy," Choker says, realizing he should not judge and be agreeable. "Where are the bases?"

"Automatics! When the ball is hit, there are designated areas for a single, double, triple and home run," Babe says. "This way, the Babe... I never had to run. Never in my life. There are no bases, so there is no running.

"Now that we are all in our 80's, the game is even more perfect for us," the pitcher says. "We don't have to do anything but hit the ball and pitch."

"And the game is quick," Babe says. "A swing and a miss and yer out. Two foul balls and yer out... one second chance... just one... none of this keep giving and giving."

"How come we never heard of it?" Cresty asks, flipping a 70-year-old or so bat in her hands. "I grew up in Drexel Hill, right across the river, and we had row homes, but we didn't play halfball."

"The game lost its popularity when families began moving out of the cities and into the suburbs in the 1950s and 1960s," the outfielder says. "I'd bet your pop never even played halfball."

"My pop? Pete?" Cresty laughs. "Not even Pete could've thought of something this brilliant."

Cresty knees Choker in the back of his knee, as if to get going.

"Now a days," the pitcher says, "just finding pimple balls is the problem.

"Years ago, I went to several stores here in South Jersey to buy pimple balls and none of the store employees even knew what I was talking about. I finally had to go online and research halfball and found someone who sold them in South Philadelphia."

"So, since we don't lose the balls, we don't need to buy them," Babe says. "And we even find some of the old balls lost when we were kids.

"Sometimes the wind blows the balls Babe hit for homers off the roofs," the outfielder says. "Like earlier today, the south breeze blew a halfball from the weeds over there and just a few minutes ago, the west wind blew a halfball from the tree behind home plate."

"What, where is a home run?" Cresty asks.

"Over the street, on the roof," the pitcher says. "But you can catch the halfball off the wall or house and yer out."

"Babe once caught the pimple ball after it hit a bird over the house," the outfielder says, pointing above the MLK House.

"Do you know who once lived in that house?" Cresty asks.

"Yeah, Babe was born there," the pitcher says.

"We heard Martin Luther King lived there," Cresty says.

"Oh yeah, the great man did," Babe says. "After I was born. It was in 1950."

"Yeah, he was a quiet man, just mostly coming home at night to do his homework from Rutgers, which was called the College of South Jersey back then," the pitcher adds. "So, we were surprised when he came home one night and was upset after he was refused service at a bar in Maple Shade.

"Now it is the local activists who are upset. The duplex has been empty, for decades. The city has it on the demo list, but the activist keep fighting it."

"We're hoping the city knocks it down ... so we have a larger field," Babe says.

"Want to play?"

"Our three sons were supposed to be here by now to play... they stop on their break from work to play... they work till sunset in the summer."

"Thanks. But we have to keep going on our ways," Cresty says.

"Thanks, too, for the history lesson," Choker says.

"And the halfball lesson," Cresty adds.

"But I do have a question," Choker says as Cresty knees him in the back of the knee again. "Although your field will be larger, won't tearing down the MLK house take away his memory?

"Is the house on the National Register of Historic Places?"

"The major street through the city is named after him and nothing has changed since he has lived here," the outfielder says softly. "Change is a c*himera* here.

"You mean something that exists only in the imagination," Choker says. "I learned that word earlier walking around."

"You learned it from Ruby and Cliff," Cresty says to him. "We need to be heading back there... to the porch."

"That is the *dissonance*... the change isn't coming from his old boarded up house," the pitcher

THE CHESS GAME

adds.

"I see now the lack of agreement," Choker says. "I learned it, I should say."

"Some say the house must stay up for *dogmatic* reasons," Babe says.

"Yup. For their own personal beliefs," Choker adds, "as if they can't be doubted, or questioned."

"The house is *specious*," Babe adds.

"It doesn't look that large," Choker says.

"Specious with an *e*," Babe corrects him. "The house is still here for a false appearance. The house doesn't need to be here."

"Not even for lessons?" Choker asks.

"Not even for lessons," Babe says. "Rising is the only lesson… finding your own *ways* is the lesson only you can learn."

"Yeah, we have to keep going on our ways," Choker says. He turns on his phone and continues singing Pride in the Name of Love:

> Early morning, April four
> Shot rings out in the Memphis sky
> Free at last, they took your life
> They could not take your pride
> In the name of love
> What more in the *game* of love
> In the name of love

What more in the blame of love
In the name of love
What more in the shame of love
In the name of love
Many more in the name of love

Three white-outfitted workers in a white double-cab pickup truck stop at the MLK House. We hear them say, "hi pops" to their three dads as we wander up the block on Eighth Street. We stop to look back on the corner of Eighth and Walnut where there is an old church with three new doors in the front. But windows on the Friendship Baptist Church, like the MLK House, are also boarded up. One block down is the Crystal Lounge with its door open.

The homeless looking man in the L. L. Bean vest wearing mirror sunglasses and the Abe Lincoln black stovepipe top hat seems to be looking out the door, as if he is guarding his empty shopping cart.

Two guys in gray suits are on the stoop playing dice. Only one guy is rolling the dice as he gets his black shoes shined by another man, who stops to pour polish on his white towel, but the bottle is empty. The other guy in the gray suit doesn't have shoes. Just socks. He just sits and stares.

THE CHESS GAME

"Do you play the chess game," Choker asks. "The game of chess?" the man getting his shoes shine asks.

"He doesn't take chances," the shoeshine man says while flicking the tips of the man toes, making due with a dry towel. "He just plays the game he knows."

"I just play dice," the man getting his shoes shine adds.

A New Jersey transit bus, with a sign for a community care on the side, stops in front of us. No one gets on.

One of the men in the yellow jackets, with the slogan KEEPING CAMDEN CLEAN AND SAFE on the bottom, Caesar, the one who sandblasted the cathedral and was berating us, gets off the bus. Pointing at the side of the bus, he says, "No community involvement since MLK went to Rutgers University, formerly the College of South Jersey, in 1950 until 1971 when sections of downtown were looted during racial riots after the beating death of a Puerto Rican by city police."

Walking backwards, Caesar goes into the Crystal Lounge, possibly to change his fortune, joining the homeless looking man looking at the empty shopping cart. Choker tries to get a look at his face, but the sandblaster Caesar blocks his view. He sticks out his hand to the man with the Abe Lincoln hat and says, "Render to Caesar what is Caesar's and render to God what is God's."

Cliff calls:

"Not long after the USS Indy was sunk, US intelligence intercepted a message from the Japanese torpedo sub that said it had sunk the Indy. But it was ignored. Still, did I say at the Inquiry, the captain was asked if he was zigzagging?"

Eighth Street suddenly turns into a one-way street. We look back to see where the street changed to one-way, even though we are walking. We didn't see a sign. Choker points to the clock on the City Hall tower, which says it's 4:44.

"We should play the number," Choker says. "Pete loved the Number 44."

"Yeah, but it is an hour behind," Cresty says.

We make a right on Kaighns Avenue. Two blocks down is an abandoned factory on Seventh Street.

Cliff texts: Qd2 Nf3. Choker seems to study the move for a minute as Cresty knees him in the back of his knee.

We look back over to the abandoned factory and the man wearing mirror sunglasses and the tan L. L. Bean vest jacket is next to Caesar, who holds the sign "The Wizard will fix everything" with one

THE CHESS GAME

hand and his other hand is out and his palm is up.

THE CHESS GAME

Chapter 13

With no king, no chess piece, to be found at the M.L. King College House and with even less of a game plan to find the Wizard now than when we started, we wander back toward City Hall. After passing the hospital, we hear gentle music floating from a red door, three-story brick house on 330 Dr. Martin Luther King Jr. Boulevard. We make a left toward the river.

A hand-written cardboard sign in the first-floor window of the house tells us we are at another historic home.

The front steps of the Walt Whitman House face the yellowish-brown brick building where two women are pushing strollers outside the barb-wired walls. The upstairs windows of the landmark house stare straight across at the glass slot peek holes of the jail's second floor.

Once again, we see the teenage girl in a catholic high school uniform of a white top and a plaid green skirt. This time she walks directly over to us with her nose up and walks up the steps of the Whitman House. She stitched the hole in her black stocking near the bottom of the hem of her dress

"Did you find PATCO?" Choker asks.

Yes, sorry I was in a hurry before," she says

overly polite. "My mom got locked up yesterday. She got caught stealing at work to pay for her heroin addiction... after, even after twice being revived with Narcan, twice, two separate times... and I'm staying with my grandmother here, upstairs. The beds are old, but the mattress, my mattress is soft.

"I visited my mom this morning at the prison. It was my first day taking the train... "

"We're sorry," Choker and Cresty both say with competing sympathy.

The school girl sits apologetically down on the steps, as if she should've asked permission first. Another hole has been ripped in her black stockings, near the bottom of the hem of her dress.

Walt Whitman probably once sat on these steps while pondering whether the North would win the Battle of Antietam. Cresty has been thinking a lot and she asks, "Is this house, I mean, is this here home on the National Register of Historic Places?"

Choker replies, "If it is, it probably is the only one that dissects the middle of a modern prison."

"The American Poet died in this row home," the girl says while looking at the jail. "His ghosts, though, are in his words and not in haunting visions proclaimed by prisoners looking out from their slotted windows toward where W.W. gasped his final breath. I have no friends, so I read a lot. I know he planned his Camden burial and designed his own mausoleum inside these brick walls that nurtured his witty wisdom.

"There are no leaves and no grass on this concrete stoop or inside the barb wire fence over there," she says with an odd relief of a sigh, as if she finally told someone what was rattling inside her head.

We hesitate to go inside with the girl.

Our follower, the homeless looking man in the L.L. Bean vest, is leaning his head against the stoop of the Whitman's house when we open the red door. This allows us to see our reflections off of his mirror sunglasses. His shopping cart is parked off to the side of the steps. It is in front of the shuttered green door of the crumbling attached house next-door. There is a pile of old mail stuffed in a flower pot on its cracked steps. The man slides to the other stoop.

We keep our distance while standing on the threshold.

While looking up straight at us through the mirror sunglasses and without shielding his face, the man says, "There is never more time for inception than there is now... there is never more time for perfection than there is now." Then he bounces up to his feet, grabs the cart and dashes up MLK toward the hospital.

He stops in front of a stand-alone row home that sells bail bonds.

"Can I use your Number seven jersey to trade for freedom?" he turns around and yells. "Did you know in the Book of Revelation there are seven churches, seven angels, seven seals and seven plagues?

"Did you know there are seven mountain summits I want to climb?"

The caretaker at the Walt Whitman House opens the first door on the left in the thin hallway. She fixes her old-fashioned glasses upright on her nose as she asks her granddaughter if she told us "how Walt suffered a stroke in the spring of 1873 when he was visiting his mom in Camden from his residence in Washington."

"With his health failing and with Lincoln gone from the nation's capital, he stayed in Camden with his brother on neighboring Stevens Street for the next 11 years. Then he bought this house on what was then called Mickle Street," the girl adds. "He used the money from the proceeds of 'Leaves of Grass'" to purchase it.

THE CHESS GAME

"There was a public viewing at the house," the caretaker lady says. "You would've waited for over an hour to stand where you are now."

With the door half open, she looks approvingly back down the main hallway of the house. On the side wall by the steps is a portrait of a seated Walt Whitman. He wears a long white beard and he is looking up admiringly at a young dark-haired and mustached man. There is a slight smile on the man's face, somewhat like the Mona Lisa smirk.

"Who is the young dude?" Choker asks.

"Peter Doyle. He was Mr. Whitman's... friend," she says, catching herself.

"You can say it," the girl says to her grandma.

"Peter Doyle was at Ford's Theater on Good Friday, April 14, 1965, the night Abraham Lincoln was assassinated during the performance of "My American Cousin," she says rapidly.

She fixes her glasses again and looks down the hall again, as if envisioning what the scene that day looked like.

"Over a thousand folks showed up in three hours," the lady adds. "Now there are just three of you."

"Three?" Choker asks.

"Yes, she is carrying," the lady says, nodding toward Cresty and me.

215

"Carrying what?" Choker asks.

"Her face says so," the lady says. "Mr. Whitman learned to read's folks faces first, before listening to their words and writing his."

"Romero's Funeral was a bit larger than Walt's final march," Cresty says quickly to avoid talk about her while nervously unfolding the pamphlet. "There were 250,000 mourners from around the globe, it says here.

"The Cardinal, a delegate from Pope John Paul II, eulogized him, saying, 'his blood will give fruit to brotherhood, love and peace.'

"But at the funeral, shots were fired, and bombs exploded. There were 31 killed.

"The violence was attributed to the government security forces."

"Big brother," the lady says, nodding suggestively through the walls and in the general direction of the homeless man with the mirror sunglasses, the Abe Lincoln black stovepipe top hat, and the shopping cart. She is right. He is still standing near the corner of the block, holding up his cardboard sign: "The Wizard will fix everything."

"Who is the Wizard?" Cresty asks the lady. "Did Walt know who was the Wizard?"

"Oh yeah," the lady whispers.

THE CHESS GAME

"Where is the Wizard?" Choker demands. She gives a look as if to come back later. He turns on his phone when she doesn't answer his second inquiry. He sings U2's Wake Up Dead Man as we leave, and the lady shuts the door.

>Jesus, Jesus *save* me
>I'm a *drone* in this world
>And a *foo-ked* up world it is too
>Tell me, tell me the story
>The one about eternity
>And the way it's all gonna be
>Wake up wake up *bread* man
>Wake up wake up *bearded* man

We head toward the homeless looking man. We know more about Walt Whitman, a dead man, now than him. Why is he wearing mirror sunglasses? Why the sign tucked in the L.L Bean vest. How come he is pushing the empty shopping cart? He shuffles away from us. Why is he carrying the Abe Lincoln black stovepipe top hat in his right hand**?**

>Jesus, I'm *dying* here boss
>I know you're looking out for us
>But maybe your hands aren't free
>Your Father, He made the world *uneven*

Is it the same in Heaven
Will you put in a word for me
Wake up wake up **f**eared man
Wake up wake up dead man

"Who are you?" Choker yells to the man. "Let me see your face?"
    The man sings the rest of the song:
        Listen to your words they'll tell you what to do
        Listen over the rhythm that's confusing you
        Listen to the *need* in the *cacophony*
        Listen over the hum in *life's rodeo*
        Listen over sounds of *bodies* in rotation
        Listen through the traffic and *over-population*
        Listen as hope and peace *kneel* to *crime*
        Listen over marching bands playing *political chime*

Choker and the man both sing:

    Wake up wake up dead man

Choker sings alone:

    Shake up Shake up Zen men

THE CHESS GAME

Humming out loud, the man turns right, walking to the rhythmic beat of his own sounds, down Haddon Avenue toward the hospital. Although the traffic light is working, an ambulance is stuck behind a road construction crew.

Again, Choker sings alone:

> Jesus, *are* you just around the corner?
> *Will* you think to try and warn her?
> Or are you *sleeping* on *nothing* new?
> *Is* there's an order in all of this disorder
> Is *life just a hate* recorder?
> Can we *re-find love* just once more?
> Wake up wake up *instead* man
> Wake up wake up dead man

At Broadway and Stevens Street, on the next block up, a family of three is hugging… and crying… walking out of the red brick Ronald McDonald's house.

"Bono and the boys, I think," Cresty says, "are becoming unhinged in the way they talk about God."

"How?" Choker asks, looking ahead. Cresty is also looking ahead, surely waiting for the empty shopping cart to poke out from around the corner.

"Asking Jesus to wake up," she says. "Asking Jesus to show himself, I guess, their faith is wavering. Bono needs a sign. Something. A symbol to show that Jesus is walking with him through the city streets."

"Don't we all," Choker declares.

"Do we?" Cresty asks. "Or is Bono unhinging?"

"Or understanding," Choker says.

Looking at the three-story, red brick Ronald McDonald House from this side of the street we can't see the hospital, but we see Doctor Knight, the anesthesiologist, coming out of the eight-story parking garage. He is stumbling toward Wali. Then, before falling, he slumps toward him, putting one arm around his shoulders, before they walk one block down to the chess game.

We can see the four little children's figures holding hands on the roof of the Ronald McDonald house above the sobbing family below.

"You would think the king would be at a house that helps kids with cancer," Choker says.

"You mean the Wizard," Cresty says.

Ruby calls.

"Where is you be at?"

"McDonalds," Choker says.

"Pick me up two chee'burgers," he demands.

"No, *the* Ronald McDonald House," Cresty

THE CHESS GAME

says.

"Pick me up two chee'burgulars then," Ruby laughs.

"The Ronald McDonald House has sheltered thousands of families since the early 1970's, providing comfort for moms and dads as their kids underwent cancer treatment," Cliff says into the phone. "You can say The Ronald McDonald House has saved lives, no doubt since positive feelings flowed from there to the hospital.

"Ironically, a man who threw way his fortune was the savior. He saved the kids, the former Eagles owner Leonard Tose did by building the happy house. But Tose, a gambler down in Atlantic City, died broke and a pauper in a hotel room across the river in Philadelphia."

Across the street from Ronald McDonald House, the pregnant lady in the short skirt walks out of the parking lot of the new Rand Transit Center with the empty Gatorade bottle. The trains and buses buzz on by the parking facility with half the seats filled.

Cliff texts: Qd5 Nb4

"I can't follow these chess moves," Choker complains. "It's like trying to make sense of this city."

"We're learning the streets, though," Cresty

says, rubbing me "And we are all getting good, healthy exercise, bro. Maybe we can start playing basketball again, well, in six months or so, by Christmas."

"Maybe Jesus, himself, will show up at the chess game," Choker says.

Cliff calls: "The USS Indy rescue didn't begin until four days after she was sunk. Four days! Of the almost 900 men in the water, only about 300, I think 316, survived. I think it was exactly 316, I remember reading because it was like the proverb 3:16 – God sent his only Son."

"The number saved was 317," Ruby chimes. "Just like St. Patrick's Day… when we used to get off work because the foreman was Irish."

"Yeah, we celebrated March 17 working in Cherry Hill, but not Martin Luther King Day," Cliff says.

"No matter, I'd learned to play old Danny Boy on me guitar," Ruby boasts. "Ruby did so on St. Paddy's Day."

"As for the USS Indy, the pilots who spotted the floating men began dropping rubber rafts," Cliff says. "Hours later… the Cecil J. Doyle arrived … the first rescue boat."

"Msgr. Michael Doyle has been rescuing South Camden for the last 40 years at Sacred Heart,"

THE CHESS GAME

Ruby boasts again, strumming his guitar in the background.

"Oh, Danny Boy," he sings. "The pipes, the pipes are calling… from land to Camden… and down to Ironside… in Fairview… where Cliffy lives."

The teenage kid in the rainbow-colored hoodie and burnt tan-yellow construction boots cuts across Broadway Avenue at MLK. He approaches the guy with black shoes without laces, black pants and wearing a black and white jacket. The guy is carrying his red backpack and is crossing Broadway the other way. They exchange the backpack as the clock on City Hall strikes 5 o'clock… but it is a lazy hour behind.

The River LINE is broken down in the middle of Martin Luther King Boulevard. The shiny white and blue train - with the words on the side of Rutgers: PRESTIGE. REPUTATION. LOCATION. VALUE. - shakes when it starts up and passes a new cop car on the corner. The cop car has its lights on to allow a lady wearing a doctor's smock and a ripped short skirt to cross. She turns around and walks down the street and enters the new CVS store. She comes out with a handful of plastic shopping bags and goes into the TD Bank on the corner. She comes out with a handful of pens.

"If you see my husband leaving the hospital," she says to the cop. "Tell him I have some stuff to sell now."

An orange traffic cone is flat, knocked over in the middle of MLK Boulevard. The cone is supposed to be re-directing traffic, but now it is just blocking cars. When a car hits it, the cone pops up. Immediately, a white van used for driving the elderly also hits the cone and it gets stuck under the van's bumper.

The van driver continues on down the road and stops in front of The Walt Whitman House. The curious old people exit the van and go inside the house where Walt Whitman died.

The teenage kid in the rainbow-colored hoodie and burnt tan-yellow construction boots hops into the van with the red backpack.

We continue down MLK before making a left at Haddon Avenue. Cooper Hospital is on our right and it is getting closer to picture time for me. We walk a block and stand across from the Camden County Police building.

"The police are... must be doing a fine, fine job," Cresty says. "We feel safe."

We look back and can see only the top floors of the prison in the middle of this city that is the poorest in the country with the highest crime rate per capita. We see faces looking out of the window slots. And we see the women with the two strollers talking to the lady wearing the doctor's smock and the ripped short skirt. "My son, my baby boy," she wails toward the prison, flapping her baggy doctor's smock and plastic shopping bags.

We enter McDonalds. We buy two *chee'burgers* for Ruby. We sit and suck down warm plastic bottles of water. Cresty gulps a third one. "I'm too nervous to eat," she says to Choker, who downs two hamburgers without eating the rolls.

In the drive-thru line, the teenage kid in the rainbow-colored hoodie and burnt tan-yellow construction boots hops out of the van. Looking at the overhead mirror attached to the building, Choker sees he leaves his red backpack in the front seat.

Choker runs over to the van. He knocks on the driver's door. The man turns. He has a fresh scar on his right cheek.

"Your friend left his backpack," Choker says to the red hair man with the scar face.

The van driver orders his food.

"Your friend," Choker says to him again, "left his backpack."

The driver says, "Listen, years ago, I was in

Ireland... vacationing in Donegal and on the ride to Derry the tour van stopped at Belleek. The old people got out to see the crystal factory. I asked the tour leader if I could take the van up north in the mountains. He told me to be back in an hour and a half.

"I drove for 45 minutes and turned around. But right before the turnaround it started getting windy and snow flurries were landing. I saw this guy carrying a big black bag.

"On the way back, I asked him if he wanted a ride. He jumped in and thanked me, putting the big black bag between the seats. We started talking and soon enough we were like old brothers. His name was Paddy."

"Paddy and I hit it off," he continues between swallows of French fries. "He invited me to his daughter's wedding in August. I told him I would be there. Then I asked him, 'what was in the big black bag?' He looked at me with disfavor and said 'none of your business.'

"We drive a few miles and I say, 'Paddy, sorry about asking about the big black bag, but...' and he interrupted and stared me in the eyes and said, 'none of your business.'

"A few blocks before we get to the crystal factory, at a stop sign, I turn to Paddy and say,

THE CHESS GAME

'really, I'm sorry…' when he turns away from me and says, 'none of your business' and hops out of the van.

"I was pretty shook. I pulled into the factory parking lot and just sat. I was glad when the old people started coming out. When the tour driver came to the door, I hopped over the seat… kicking the big, black bag… Paddy left his big, black bag."

Choker says, "So what was in the big, black bag?"

"None of your business," he says.

"But."

"None," he says, "of your business."

THE CHESS GAME

Chapter 14

The dipping sun's reflection splashes back toward us off the green glass of the tallest skyscraper in Philly after reflecting off the backs of smaller buildings in front of the steel giant. The angle of the light reflects on the other tall buildings, making the structures below William Penn all shine like Philadelphia is indeed Emerald City.

With our eyes squinting, we walk down the repaved section of Haddon Avenue and we admire the view across the river. That's where the Declaration of Independence was signed, we all think as we're on our way, finally, to Cooper Hospital.

"The hospital started as just a maternity hospital," says a woman in workout gear. A backpack with metal weights inside the sagging sack rattles as she jogs in place. "That's when kids were being born in the city... and not in the suburbs. Now people are flown back to the city... to die... to finish up here like Walt Whitman did... to die with the city."

Looking east, at an oval, a revised traffic circle in the middle of the road, there is a gargantuan warehouse-fortress looking building facing us. The woman tells us that this building once housed the old Camden Armory and that after the war the huge open area inside was used as an arena. She said over 5,000 fans could sit inside and watch basketball games. This perked up Cresty's interest. However, it seems like she is slowing down. She must be dead tired.

"The four high schools in town - Camden, Camden Catholic, St. Joseph's and Woodrow Wilson - used to play their basketball games in there," she says. It was called "The City Series." But in the early 1960s Camden Catholic moved to the suburbs in Cherry Hill following the Courier-Post to an open space across Cuthbert Boulevard, and St. Joseph's was closed in 1979. It is now an old age home.

"What remained in the city, as far as high schools go, is Camden and Wilson. If you call that remaining. They graduate less than half of their students despite the spending for each student is among the highest in New Jersey.

"Thankfully, the state took over the city school system a few years ago," the woman says, adjusting her weighted backpack. "There is hope."

Cliff text the chess moves: Qxb7 O-O

"What do the letters mean?" she asks, looking at Choker's phone.

THE CHESS GAME

"Don't know," he says. "I just play along in their game."

"We know," Cresty injects, "we know what they are, moves in a chess game, but we don't know where the pieces are in the game."

"Like Camden," the woman says while jogging in place.

She adjusts the weights in her backpack again.

"The old Armory is now the city of Camden's Department of Public Works," she says.

"I'd say the three-story, red brick building with its slanted bird-stained roof needs work," Cresty chuckles, the only one laughing at her own joke.

Choker flips the screen on his phone from the chess moves to his music. As Cresty fakes like she is surfing, he sings U2's Every Breaking Wave:

> Every breaking wave on the shore
> Tells the next one there'll be one more
> And every *drinker* knows that to *booze*
> Is what you're really there for
> *Bummer… many homeless*
> Now I speak *to answer of groan*
> Like every fallen leaf on the breeze
> Winter wouldn't *find them a home*
> Alone
> *Nowhere to* go

KEVIN CALLAHAN

If you go your way and I go mine

The woman jogs in place again, lifting her knees even higher. Her weights rattle. She says: "Alone. We all go on our *ways* alone, in the end."
Choker circles. His paces are steady. He is in a groove. His methodic circle suddenly widens and with each step fades, drifts further away from her. He continues to sing:

> Are we so
> Are we so helpless against the tide
> Baby, every dog on the street
> Knows that we're *just shoved* with defeat
> Are we ready to be swept off our *street*
> And stop chasing every breaking wave
> Every sailor knows that the sea
> Is a friend made enemy
> And every shipwrecked soul knows what it is
> To live without *certainty*
> I thought I heard the captain's voice
> But it's hard to listen while you *search*
> Like every broken wave on the shore
> This is as far as I could reach
> *No where to* go
> If you go your way and I go mine
> Are we so…

THE CHESS GAME

The woman tucks in her chin and picks up her pace jogging in place, knees even higher, running to be alone. She leaves in the middle of the song.

"Bono is getting like Jesus, I feel, talking in parables, using paradoxes," Cresty explains, biting the bottom of the right side of her lip. "Like in Every Breaking Wave how... I mean, how to really believe, you need to stop looking for new signs from God to believe. Just believe because you believe."

"You mean like a lady with her feet always moving and weights in her backpack?" Choker asks.

"Exactly, bro," Cresty says so fast that she spits. "Stop looking for miracles..."

Exaggerating a slow-motion run in place, Choker continues singing:

> Are we so helpless against *mankind*
> Baby, every *dude* on the street
> Knows that we're *all shoved* with defeat
> Are we ready to be swept off our *street*
> And stop chasing every breaking wave
> Our G... knows where are the *cracks*
> And drowning is no sin
> You know where *our hearts swim*
> The same place that *sores* have been

And we know that we fear to win
And so we end before we begin
Before we *sin*

"Sounds like Bono is figuring faith out is his own head, in his own words... with the help of your words, maybe on his own manageable terms," Cresty reasons with self-satisfaction and not judgment. "He isn't looking for Jesus to show up on the corner every day.
"But he is looking."
"I'm still looking for Him," Choker says. "I think Jesus understands man's search to justify our existence. After all... Jesus *was* a man, too."
Choker stops his fake running to sing:

If *we* go
If you go your *ways* and I go mine
Are we so
Are we so helpless against the tide
Baby, every *dude* on the street
Knows that we're *shoved up* with defeat
Are we ready to be swept off our feet
And stop *facing* every breaking wave

We wander past the old armory and continue east toward the suburbs. But a murky river and a

THE CHESS GAME

busy highway obstruct us, and we reverse our course back toward the city.

The rush hour bumper-to-bumper traffic is barely inching forward. The banks of the Cooper River seem to be caving into the muddy water. Suddenly, before turning back, Cresty reaches down and cups a handful of mud. She throws the wet sand in the river.

"I needed this Magnetic Reversion Reversal therapy," she says, looking out over the river and then back toward the city.

The jogger with the weighted backpack has made a loop and turns back toward us. She stops and looks into the curvy, murky river along the super highway.

She seems in a trance when she says, "The river reminds me of the Camden 28... Michael Doyle... his brilliant closing argument... comparing the law to the river."

"Go on," Cresty says, wiping her muddy hands on the grass.

"He explained to the jury how the 'Law is very useful in helping us to protect life, but law is not as good as life,'" she says deliberately, with her eyes closed, as if the words are imprinted on the back of her eyelids. "How he reasoned, 'law is the banks of the river and the water is the life. The stream flows, but the banks must widen if the stream gets fuller, the law must make room for life and not the other way around. Ever.' "

The woman, opening her eyes in a blink, adjusts the weights in her backpack and runs away... back toward the city.

Ruby calls:

"Where'd you be?"

"On Admiral Wilson *B*," Choker says cheerfully, as if the running woman's words weighted his conscience. "B as in Boulevard."

"I thought you meant B as in baby," Cresty says. Choker crunches his face.

"Did I tell ya'll, that on Admiral Wilson Boulevard, the *man* razed a half dozen strip joints 10 years ago when the Republican National Convention landed across the river in Philadelphia," Ruby says more than asks. "But you can see for yourselves how'd no new business have replaced the topless bars."

Looking ahead, the high summer sun also reflects off the glass of the sprawling modern building complex behind the old armory. The Campbell Soup building's letters of white stand out against the red background. The main building looks like a Campbell Soup can.

We walk under an overpass sheltering

THE CHESS GAME

cardboard houses along with some tents and tarps. Tent City? There is an open space in the middle of surrounding tents. The space could fit three large railroad train cars, but instead there is just a stool. A short stool on wheels. A boy with blonde bangs shooting straight under an olive-green army helmet, the canvas straps hanging from both sides, swipes at the hair dangling over the tops of his eyes as he gently spins the stool seat. His ambivalent eyes transfixed, he seems careful not to spin the seat cushion off the stool. The people sitting snug outside their living space hold their ears right before an oil tanker train rolls by on the overpass above them. The train rumbles along, going in front of Cooper Hospital and into the city, moving toward the clock on the City Hall tower, which says its 5:55.

"Should we play the number?" Cresty asks.

"Play? Yup," Choker says.

The intersection ahead of us is paved. The pavers are expensive and decorative. They match the sidewalk. Cooper University Hospital borders the fancy crossroad. The new section of Cooper is a shiny green glass structure of nine floors. Above the paved intersection there is an elevated crosswalk, which reaches like an outstretched arm from the old section of the hospital to the new

M.D. Anderson Cancer Center across the street.

The original emergency room and the two new hospital facilities seem to be just one giant medical complex on the intersection of old Martin Luther King Boulevard and Haddon Avenue.

"Maybe the king is here at the hospital, right where we started this morning," Choker says.

"You mean the Wizard," Cresty says.

"Well, I mean, damn... what do I mean?" Choker says.

Up ahead, there is a sign: COOPER PLAZA HISTORIC HOMES. Even though it is green, we stop at the traffic light just to stare at the overpass wall decorated with photos, well paintings, of two men.

Even with all the knowledge they boast, Choker, and Cresty don't know who they are. They don't bother to walk across the street to read the small letters below each painting that would reveal the identities. Perhaps because a man wearing a Santa Claus hat is... well, pissing on the wall between the portraits of the two men who are wearing ties. Perhaps, they are tired of walking.

"Who are those men?" Cresty asks the jogger with the weighted backpack, who rushed up behind us.

"Well, the one guy is Summer Santa," she says. "He generously waters the flowers on the ramps of the overpass.

"No. Not him. The two portraits," Choker demands. "Perhaps Clarence Turner? I know its not Walt Whitman and his friend, I know what they look like."

"Not Nipper the Dog either," Cresty says. "They have to be somebody that made a difference."

"Don't know, but I do know the hospital's spokesperson is the pretty Kelly Ripa," the woman says, jogging in place again. We don't hear the weights rattling since we are all transfixed on the paintings in such an unusual spot. "Maybe they are just… people. not pretty ones or ugly ones."

There is rattling from above. We look over to see if the oil tanker derailed over the Cardboard City and onto the homes of the homeless.

"Looks like the hospital has a heliport on the roof," Choker discovers, pointing skyward.

"Cooper is the regional trauma center," the woman says. "All the injured and the hopelessly dying, come in from the suburbs. Just like the leafy towns send their garbage to South Camden to burn in the trash-to-steam plant. That plant stinks up the neighborhood, Waterfront South, where Sacred Heart parish was rebuilt by Father Doyle after the acquittal of the Camden 28."

"Miss, you are like Wikipedia on wheels," Choker says, barely causing her to break stride as she continues to run in place.

"At the trial, in his closing argument, he told the jury the trial was simply about one thing: Truth. Father Doyle said, "George Bernard Shaw said, 'Christ is killed in every generation for those who don't have imagination.'"

She goes on, "I would say that justice starts with each one of us. My mom brought me to the closing argument of Father Doyle. I remember the windows were open on the fourth floor of the Courthouse and the wind was blowing the curtains out the window and blowing my long hair. My mom exposed me at the age of 12 to social justice. Expose your child to social justice... teach your child to have an imagination.

"My mom told me, rather implored me, saying 'it is up to you to live an interesting life.'"

We look up again as the helicopter lifts off. Staring as the flying ambulance floats back east, back toward the suburbs. Looking down, we notice that we are being followed again. The homeless looking man pushes the empty shopping cart onto the concrete paver oval outside of Cooper Hospital. The jogger looks into his mirror sunglasses, rubs some mud off her face that Cresty must have sprayed onto her, and puts her weighted backpack into the shopping cart.

We are an hour early to meet with Dr. Burk. We see him through a glass door pacing in circles around a short stool with a padded cushion, clutching a thick American Revolutionary War textbook in his right hand while talking on his phone in his left. Both hands are trembling.

He finally comes out when the clock in the waiting room says it is 8:06.

We do the ultrasound.

The photograph says I'm alive.

"The heart beat is strong," the doc says. "Your blood work is fine, very normal. Like I said, the heartbeat is strong. See, look at the photograph."

"I know," Cresty says.

"You knew the whole time?" Choker asks. "I didn't even know... why didn't you tell me?

"If I did, we wouldn't have made this senseless... wild... wonderful wander through Ruby's city," Cresty says.

"We wouldn't have been stalked by a man pushing a shopping cart," Choker protests.

"That's why I didn't tell you."

"I wouldn't have searched for the meaningless king, or play this even more meaningless chess game," he says, raising his voice in front of the perplexed doctor.

"You mean the Wizard," she smiles. "And isn't it the Game of Chess?"

Holding hands, we walk under the red Cooper flags that hang on the new streetlamps that have been made to look old.

Choker and Cresty – we - stroll north on Haddon Avenue toward City Hall and make a left down MLK toward the river. We stop at the three-story red brick Ronald McDonald House. Choker glances over to the eight story-parking garage. We sit on the bench near the statue of another family of four hugging below the four little kid's figures holding hands on the roof.

The man wearing a Santa Claus hat stops near us on the street and reads out of a book. He says, "There is a medical library in the hospital. We needed it since the Cooper Library almost closed a few years ago before being incorporated by the county. Like the police.

"Now both the library and the police are better than ever. I can read safely on the street downtown here."

"And piss on walls," Choker laughs, "without getting it shot off.

"I should've got mine shot off…"

"Then Oscar Romero would be happy with the police here," Cresty says to Santa, interrupting

Choker. "Especially after the investigations into his assassination revealed nothing... no one has ever been prosecuted for the death of the martyr."

The chugging oil tanker train churns back over the overpass. It is loaded, now going from the city to the suburbs. Smoke from the huffing engine floats and lands on the green bushes and grass around the hospital and around the portraits on Cooper Plaza.

Behind us, we hear the roar of cars on 676 and then in the background we hear the weighted shopping car being pushed over the red and white brick paved crosswalk. Then onto the cobblestones of Seventh Street and then to the cobblestones on Chambers Street.

We barely hear Choker's phone chime.

"The USS Indy, "Cliff says over the speakerphone.

"Huh?" Choker says. "Can't hear you over the cacophony of Camden."

Cliff continues talking, though, at the same level, adding "was assumed safe, which is why the Navy failed to learn of her sinking. The admirals who were plotting the positions on the big board with incoming reports weren't alarmed when no one, or no other ships saw the Indy.

"The Navy just assumed the big boat would reach its destination."

With no sound of the squeaky wheels, we look back for the shopping cart man wearing an Abe Lincoln black stovepipe top hat. Instead, we see the man wearing the Santa Claus hat standing next to the statue at the Ronald McDonald House. He wipes his hands on the furry cap and throws it in the gutter. He lies down next to the Santa hat.

The jogger, running faster and looking lighter without the weighted backpack, jumps over the Santa in disguise. She stops and picks up the Santa hat and puts it on her head.

"There is hope for Camden, too," she says, or rather proclaims. "Just a few months after the jury nullification for Father Doyle and the Camden 28, the United States ended the conflict in Vietnam."

THE CHESS GAME

Chapter 15

An idling New Jersey Department of Transportation utility truck blocks the right lane of traffic on MLK Boulevard as a DOT worker in an orange hoodie jaywalks across Broadway Avenue, fumbling with a large orange juice container.

The lady in the doctor's smock and ripped short skirt is walking in circles on the corner inside the truck's ring of exhaust. As we wander towards them, she invites Choker back to her "Cardboard City," pointing east and back toward the suburbs to under the overpass. Seeing no reaction and hearing no response from Choker, she starts pointing toward the Rand parking garage... we think she says, "A *grand* parking garage."

We agree. "Yes, a grand garage," Choker and Cresty say at once.

"No. No, no. The prison is safe for my son," she says, pointing beyond the garage and to the upper floors of the jail. "No drugs in there for him to do. And I'm safe in my Cardboard City, close to him, close to *my* baby.

"Have you seen my husband yet? Dr. Knight?"

Rubbing Cresty's belly, the lady sings to us, "Baby, baby, baby, light my way."

Benson Street is one-way going toward the river

and into a dead end at the medical building on Broadway, the newly built Cooper Medical School of Rowan University.

A construction worker wearing Carhartt overalls is sitting on the steps of the new building.

"Can I stay here if the city knocks down Tent City?" he asks. "Can I have your Number seven jersey if all my clothes are taken, too?

"You know, the apostle Paul refers to Jesus with seven titles..."

"I thought it was called Cardboard City?" Choker asks him.

"You are right," the construction man says. "On sunny days like today it is Cardboard City, but on rainy days, the cardboard sags, so the tents get crowded in Tent City."

The lady wrapped in a ripped short skirt and wearing a doctor's smock pokes the construction workers chest. She snaps his overall straps and says, "Cardboard City will never be... can't never be... won't never be... Tent City without George Washington's tent."

"You mean," the construction worker replies politely while holding her hand against his chest, "*the* George Washington?"

"Yes," she answers flipping her hand over his. "*General* George."

"*Revolutionary War* George, yes" he agrees

THE CHESS GAME

with satisfaction. "Yes, ma'am."

She wiggles her hand free from his chest, reaches under her smock and pulls out a folded paper. Carefully unfolding what appears to be a ripped page from a textbook, she points to a photo of an oval shaped white tent with red trim. The tent top is pointed by two poles spread out in the middle.

"This is General Washington's Tent," she whispers sacredly, pointing to the photo. "He lived with his troops during the Revolutionary War... lived in the mud and the fields... slept and dined in the freeze of Valley Forge."

"He did, yes ma'am," the construction worker nods.

"We need another revolution in this country and a general who will lead us from the king's tyranny," she says shaking the photo. "My husband worked in the hospital with another Doc who said his great grandfather was the pastor at Annunciation Church in Gloucester, just off of King Street by the waterfront, who bought the handed-down tent a hundred years after the war to preserve as a symbol and a reminder that our leaders should live with the people like General George lived with his troops.

"The doctor, Doc Burk," she continues, the annoyance peaking in her voice, "says he is in a legal tango with the founders who plan to build an American Revolutionary War Museum across the river in Philadelphia, near where the Declaration of

Independence was signed... but the tent shouldn't be staged in a building when the war isn't over... when the revolution hasn't revolved."

"Yes ma'am."

"Now there is just a stool there," she says sadly. "A stool waiting for a piano... hoping for us it's the George Washington piano."

"Yes ma'am..." the construction worker says and then looking toward the overpass asks, "why can't we build the American Revolutionary War Museum over here... here in Camden?"

"The tent," Choker declares while kneeling on his right knee and then singing like Bono, "Could be the Angel of Camden."

We wander. We follow a tasty smell up Benson to where a vendor is boiling, sending steam into the air, drifting toward the hospital roof. As another helicopter is landing there, he yells, "Get yer *baddest ass* dinner dogs here."

We hear the click-clack of the River LINE off in the graying distance and then a familiar rattling behind us. The homeless looking man pushing the shopping cart is back following us. The cart is empty again and the mirror sunglasses are flipped up on his head.

Choker says, "Must be having hallucinations," but I don't know if he is referring to himself or to the man in the L.L Bean jacket.

THE CHESS GAME

From the vest, the man flashes the cardboard sign. "The Wizard will fix everything" and offers a crooked smile.

An ambulance siren screams by us going up the one-way street as Choker says, "Dang lightnin' on fire." Another siren whistles by us going in the other direction, toward the river. With the street quiet again, the man flips over the cardboard sign: "If the Wizard will be the Wizard who will serve."

The man takes his sign and walks up toward Cooper Hospital. Choker steps onto the porch on Benson Street and says, "I just had a vision that I was in a brothel." Cresty says, "only your mind" and studies the chessboard.

"No, this be the Porch of Versailles," says Ruby, tapping his red sneakers.

"Mind if we watch?" Cresty asks, looking closer at the chessboard and knowing the answer.

"You'd made it back fine… right on time," Ruby says with a mighty laugh that shakes both straps on his dungaree overalls down his bony and bare shoulders.

"I can't wander anymore," Cresty says. "I'm so sleepy "

Cliff helps her to sit on his chair, moving his thick book as he adds: "Versailles means to turn over and over… like plowing fields.

"The Latin word means 'to sow'… you sow'd today."

Cresty rubs me as she goes inside the row home and lies down on the sofa near the open window.

"Did Clarence Turner die?" Choker asks emphatically.

"You'd mean the King of the Castle on the Hill?" Ruby asks.

"He lives in Chicago now with his daughter, the word on the street is," Cliff says. "Ruby used to play his guitar at his games. Tell him Ruby."

"Yeah, I'd had a lovely song. I would sit on the steps as the opposing team came into the gym and play sweetness."

"Sing it Ruby."

Ruby picks up his three-string guitar and strums along with the words:

"We'd black … you'd white … you'd win … we'd fight," he roars and then he laughs, showing off his three teeth and singing it again while strumming the same three stings.

"We'd blaaack…, you'd white … you'd win … we'd fight."

The guitar neck bends and almost snaps with Ruby laughing so mightily and leaning it against the chessboard.

"It, Ruby's song, used to make the other team

THE CHESS GAME

laugh, too" Cliff says. "No one ever fought!"

"Yeah it took the edge off coming into Camden for the pale teams from the suburbs, like Cherry Hill East and Camden Catholic," Ruby says. "That was fun back then. Do that now and they'd be locking old Ruby up."

"I heard Coach Turner had a rhyme before each game with just the team," Choker says.

"He was the Bard of Baird Boulevard, you know," Ruby says.

"But, only the team knows the chant," Cliff says.

"Well, I heard it from a janitor who used to be cleaning outside the Camden locker room for the afternoon game," Choker says.

"Say it son," Cliff says, carefully placing his book back on his chair and then sitting.

Choker says, "Johnny Luckett, mother … "

"Yeah, it was Coach Turner's *ways*," Ruby says.

"Ways? How so?" Choker asks.

"The rhyme was his ways of saying his boys wouldn't need any luck to win that here game," Ruby says, lifting his legs onto the table and allowing the red sneakers to hang over the edge and knocking over his guitar. "A man needs to mind his *ways*."

"You mean like no Rochambeau?" Cresty asks while perking up and sticking her head out the window, staring at Choker. "You hear me? No Rochambeau. No luck of the draw."

Cresty adds, "All right. *Cool gobble ghoul.*"

Tapping his red sneakers, Ruby says, "The King of the Castle on the Hill ... the Bard of Baird Boulevard ... Coach Clarence knew he'd best learn his boys to make their own *ways.*"

Pushing the shopping cart back toward us and with his mirror sunglasses still flipped up on his head, the man that looks like Choker stops in front of the porch. While pointing across the river toward Philadelphia with the setting sun shining off the reflective green-glassed high rise behind William Penn, he says, "There is Emerald City... he really must be a wonderful Wizard to live in a city glowing like that."

The man looks at Ruby's red sneakers and says, "I want those ruby slippers most of all."

Ruby gives them to him. He puts the sneakers in his shopping cart.

Choker is frozen. The man does look like him, but older. He puts the mirror sunglasses on Choker and pushes onward and away from this Victorian two-story, I mean, three-story, red brick double house on Benson here. The house was constructed to last. But the entire street has been refurbished. The bricks actually are more orange than red.

Cliff makes his move: Qxb4.

"The USS Indy," Cliff says and hesitates. He continues, "The court-martial did not blame her captain for her sinking, but the distraught families of the dead men did."

Ruby follows with his move: c5 and says, "Always, blame is needed... demanded."

"The guilt worked," Cliff says while studying Ruby's move. "He committed suicide using his Navy revolver. He shot himself on his front lawn while clutching a toy sailor of his youth in his other hand."

"Sorry," Choker and Cresty say together.

"Well, of course you are sorry," Cliff says. "Tragic."

"Sorry, but I was saying I'm sorry because I never found the king," Choker says. "I do know that, the captain's demise was tragic, of course. Cresty and I need to roll..."

"Listen," Ruby says. "Father Doyle concluded his closing argument with the Robert Frost poem, The Road Less Taken, and he said to the jurors that they, the Camden 28, took the road less taken protesting the Vietnam War ...

"He, Father Doyle, concluded by saying that

someday he'd hoped to meet up with the jurors when the road, whatever road they chose… when their roads, meet again.

"So, Ruby will see you down the road."

Cresty and I walk swiftly down to the end of the block. We walk toward the construction worker wearing Carhartt overalls who wants Choker's Number seven jersey. Choker lags behind. He is carrying Ruby's three-string guitar.

We pass the Camden Parent Partnership in the middle of the block and stop at the Center for Family Services. It is on the corner of Benson across from Rowan's new medical center.

A tall lady, redheaded with long curls, comes out of the Center for Family Services. She reaches for Cresty's pamphlet.

"He tried to stop the violence," the redheaded lady says approvingly. "Romero tried. Just like so many have tried here, his fellow catholic priests like Monsignor McDermott in East Camden at St. Joe Pro, and Monsignor Mannion at the Cathedral in Center City and, of course, Monsignor Doyle in South Camden at Sacred Heart."

The Three Monsignors," Cresty nods."

"They all tried, like Romero," the redheaded lady agrees while admiring Cresty's hair, now floating on her shoulders. "Monsignor Doyle says

THE CHESS GAME

his tombstone will read: "I failed nicely."

The clock on the City Hall tower says its 8:06… but it is an hour behind.

The parking lot attendant and the doctor barge out from a house down Benson Street a little distance from us and the redheaded lady. The house has a blue and white door next to a red fence.

Wali, the parking attendant, says with authority, "Take them to our gardens behind the Porch of Versailles,"

The lady with the long red hair like Cresty, but way more curly, walks us down an alley behind the red wooden fence to where there is a park with benches. There is a black railing in the middle of this city garden square behind Benson Street.

"In 2000, Pope John Paul II commemorated the martyrs of the 20th century in Rome's Coliseum," she says to us, placing her neck over the black railing like she is ready to be chopped, executed. "His Holiness insisted Romero be included on the list.

"Will you and I be next? Will you teach your baby?"

As Choker approaches with Wali and Dr. Knight, Cresty, not reading from the pamphlet, says, "Romero was made a saint, too, but was he a martyr because of his killer's hatred toward the

Catholic Church, or was he killed for politics, for his liberation theology movement?"

From behind us, Choker sings U2's Songs For Someone:

> You've got a face not spoiled by *society*
> I have some scars from where I've been
> You've got eyes that can see right through me
> You're not afraid of anything they've seen
> I was told that I would *steal*
> *Something* the first time
> I don't know how these cuts heal
> But in *here* I found a *fight*
> If there is *might*
> You can always see

The lady raises her head off the railing as Choker starts strumming Ruby's three-string guitar. He continues to sing:

> And there is a world
> We can *only see*
> *So where* is a spark
> That we shouldn't doubt
> *If* there is a light
> Don't let it *blow* out
> And this is a song

THE CHESS GAME

A song for someone
This is a song
A song for *no* on

The inquisitive redheaded lady with the lovely long curls is talking to Cresty. She apparently is answering her questions about Romero: "Like in the song, even when spiritual events in your life or unanswerable religious questions like about Oscar Romero don't seem to make sense for your life, they could be God's song for *someone* who you don't know."

"The event, the words, the song, could be touching *someone* in need," she adds. "Or, it could be touching a part of you that you don't *even* know yet… a part of you that might someday betray Him."

The lady rubs me. "What is your name? I say, Jude," she says. "If you ever need me… "

"You work at the Camden Family Services Center," Cresty says.

"Yeah, I work there, too," she says smiling.

Still behind us and still strumming, Choker continues singing:

You *led* me into a conversation
An intervention only we could make

You're breaking into my imagination
Whatever's in there is yours to *break*
I was told I'd *steal*
Something the first time
You were slow to heal
But this could be the night
If there is a light
You can always see
And there is a world
We *can't* always be
If there is a *rock*
Within and without
Where there is a light
Don't let it go out
And this is a song
A song for someone
This is a song
A song for *no* one
And *find* a long *ways*
From your hill on Calvary

    Harder, Choker strums Ruby's three-string guitar as he continues to sing:

    And *we're* a long way
    From where I was, where I need to be
    If there is a light

THE CHESS GAME

You *will* always see
And there is a world
We *can't* always be
If there is a kiss
I stole from your mouth
If there is a light,
Won't let it go out

The squeaking tells us the homeless man is pushing the shopping cart with Ruby's sneakers popping out the side. He rolls it into the garden.

"Hey dude," he says, turning to look at us. "I was following you today only because *we* were just recruiting, or screening you to live in our Cardboard City."

The man says, "Tent City when it rains." as Choker slides up the mirror sunglasses on his forehead and stares at him in the face. Choker flinches, realizing *just* how much he looks just like him.

Choker takes off the glasses and looking down, he gazes at his reflection in the mirrors. He then looks then back at the shopping cart man. He is not wearing the Abe Lincoln black stovepipe top hat. Neither of them offers a reaction.

"We're looking for diversity to keep our federal funding and you three are, well, one black, one white and one to be half-n-half."

He turns to Dr. Knight and says, "Your wife is looking for you back in our city."

"We were just looking for the king," Choker says. "We didn't mean to lead you on, thinking we were looking to stay."

"I thought, we thought, I think that the king was, or is, *the* Wizard," Cresty says.

"We're done looking for the king," Choker declares.

"You have to learn to not look up at the City Hall clock," the man with Choker's face says. "But look at the gold cross on the spire of the Cathedral below the clock to find the king... or as you say, *the* Wizard."

"Your sign," Cresty says, pointing inside his vest, "says *The* Wizard."

From the cart, the man without the mirror sunglasses and without the Abe Lincoln black stovepipe top hat offers Cresty both of Ruby's sneakers. He flips the cart on its side. She sits. Tugging on the tight knots, she wrestles off her sneakers and slips on Ruby's oversized sneakers. She doesn't tie them. Standing, she flips up the shopping cart and drops in her basketball sneakers with the letters P E T E printed neatly on both heels.

THE CHESS GAME

Chapter 16

Choker strums on Ruby's guitar as we wander down MLK Boulevard toward Wiggins Marina. We stand on the overpass and look down on a red and white shipping tanker anchored in the middle of the Delaware River. Then we look up to the Ben Franklin Bridge. We can see the scattered rooftops of former row homes that are now single structures in the "Forbidden Territory" north of the bridge. The steeple of the closed church rises in the middle of North Camden, just beyond the shadow of the tall "R" Building of Rutgers University.

The *whatever-name bank* music center rises to our left in front of the USS New Jersey battleship.

Choker and Cresty, well, we all plop on the huge golden ship propeller that welcomes us again to the Camden Waterfront. We are back to where the city began on the river, where the gentle ginger lady who calls me Jude had told us Monsignor Doyle said confidently years ago how the city would be reborn during a ceremony when a fishing pier was named after him near the old New York Shipbuilding yard.

Here we are... on the river.

Across this flowing water that divides Philadelphia and Camden is the Moshulu, a former four-masted steel barque that is now dry-docked.

There is a waiting line on the pier, making the "M" appear to be a popular floating restaurant

"Swim you across for dinner," Cresty says, challenging Choker.

"Don't want to get *me* new guitar soggy, but this, the river, reminds me of what Pete taught us. At least that's what I was just thinking," Choker rattles.

"Huh?"

"Remember, how Pete did tell us, how he came up with his River Religion, when, or how once on shore, you can just patch up the hole in your boat or raft, meaning your life, and then get back on the high seas or river," Choker reminds us.

"Ya," Cresty adds. "And if you had a passenger weighing your raft down, you needed to leave them, or heave them, on shore. How, without that person, whether a friend or foe, wife or girlfriend, teammate or soul mate, drinking buddy or some buddy or body you don't even really know, you just get back on your raft and float."

"Yup."

"Is that what we are doing? What we did today?" Cresty asks. "Are we patching our raft?"

"Maybe. Possibly."

"Na. We're doing more than that," Cresty determines.

THE CHESS GAME

"Yup, we're still looking for the king."

"Ya, but don't you mean The Wizard," she says laughing.

They hold hands while wandering toward the battleship moored to their left. We wander to the shore of the Delaware River. The dividing river. Ahead, there is a semi-circular boat marina. Less than half the slips are filled.

A burnt orange-colored building is locked up. A window washer with a camouflage yellow jacket and reading glasses stands in front of the grimy glass, which faces the river. A sign with painted white letters on its side tell us this is Ulysses S. Wiggins Park and Marina.

The fence protecting the ramp leading to the boats is chained, but there is enough room to slide around the gate and onto the pier.

We meet a sailor inside Wiggins Marina. We know he won't evict us since he is chugging out of a bottle wrapped in a 7-11 bag. Cresty offers him some of the mixed M&Ms from the 7-11 bag stuffed in her back pocket.

"You know kiddies, Dr. Wiggins was born on a f... f... farm in Georgia near Andersonville, which was only about 30 years or so after the infamous con... con... confederate prison was closed there," the sailor slurs. He reaches for Ruby's guitar, but

Choker curls it around behind his back. He takes a handful of M&Ms instead.

"Young Wiggins grew to serve in the Army and then went to medical school before he became a doc and came to Camden. He became very active in the Civil Rights movement," the sailor says, sounding suddenly sober. "He helped get the city schools integrated after World War II. But he failed in his attempt to win an elected office in Camden... but now he has a marina named after him... right down the street from another prison... he rests near a jail, just like near where he was born...

"Go figure."

"Maybe he is the king," Choker says.

"Ha! You mean the Wizard," Cresty says.

He throws the brown bottle into the river and stuffs the plastic 7-11 bag into his *camo* top pocket. The sailor then tells us that he is a tour guide for the Battleship New Jersey. We follow him with a bounce and a leap from the plank onto the hulking ship.

Choker and Cresty keep their heads low while walking below decks, but we still can see the "bull's-eyes" painted everywhere on the sidewalls of the ship.

"They're every four feet," the sailor says, signaling to the yellow box with black lettering and numbers. "The markings tell you where you are, what level you are on the ship."

Popping the M&Ms, he explains the first number tells how many decks below the main deck you are.

"If you can't remember all of the Navy's nomenclature, the first number tells if you have to go above or below."

Back on deck, the sailor explains that he teaches the quadratic formula, which is used to assist in firing the 16-inch guns. He said the distance the projectile is fired is factored by this formula.

"You can stay overnight onboard."

"No thanks,' Cresty says, "We must be getting back to our boat in Cape May."

"Or we can stay at Cardboard City, the Waterfront's Woodstock under the overpass," Choker reminds her.

"That reminds me when Pete took me to Woodstock one summer day when I was a little girl," she says. "We pulled up in a minivan and a leftover hippie guy came strolling over. Pete lowered the window and as the air-conditioned air hit our sweaty greeter, he said, "Welcome home man" and without missing a beat, Pete said, "Good to be back dude."

"I think you told me that story," Choker says.

The guide tells us the Battleship New Jersey, or "the *bad, bad* BB62", was built at the Philadelphia Naval Shipyard.

"Don't you mean here in Camden?" Choker asks.

"Ya, at the New York Shipyard," Cresty says.

The sailor just says, "Big J was launched Dec. 7, 1942, a year to the day after the attack on Pearl Harbor."

"A day that still lives in infamy," Choker says.

"Sadly, like Camden," Cresty laments.

"After roles in World War II, Korea, Vietnam and the Persian Gulf, the Battleship New Jersey was decommissioned in 1991 at Bremerton, Washington," the sailor says. "Then, Big J was docked there until 1999 when it was towed to the Philadelphia Naval Shipyard for restoration work. The next year she arrived at the Camden waterfront to become a permanent floating museum.

"Did you ever see a king onboard?" Choker asks our guide. "The chess piece. You know, the king."

"You mean the Wizard?" the sailor guide asks, smiling at Cresty.

After exiting the ship, Choker and Cresty meander down to the end of the refurbished pier. Choker peels off his hiking boots as Cresty flicks the untied laces of Ruby's sneakers. They hang their feet above the water. Choker lays back on the plastic pier and stares into the three-string guitar in his hands. Cresty rests her head on his chest.

The churning of a tugboat's engine, which is pushing a barge past the anchored ship, prevents them from going to sleep.

"Ulysses," Choker says suddenly.

"Yeah like Ulysses Grant." Cresty says. "The Civil War winning general."

"Might as well be, a Civil War in this city divided by the past and present, got Lincoln shot and brought the man who shot the man who shot Abe here" Choker says. "Even the Ben Franklin Bridge divides the *forgotten* city from the *forbidden* city."

"And, with fate and future divided by the river from its prosperous neighbor, Philly is the Emerald City compared to poor Camden," says Cresty.

"But it is not that Ulysses," Choker says.

"Yeah it is the doctor named Wiggins," Cresty says.

"Maybe he was named after Ulysses? Wiggins, huh?"

"The Greek?"

"Yeah, from the Odyssey," Choker says. "Remember, I was an English major my freshman year at Ursinus."

"Our freshman year," Cresty says.

"Yeah. It took Ulysses ten years to get home after the Trojan War... maybe I should've used a Trojan and we wouldn't be here."

"Have faith like Ulysses," Cresty says. "We'll get home. We'll build a home."

"Faith?"

"In God."

"But how can you have faith when God doesn't answer your prayer?"

"When didn't God listen?" Cresty asks. "Maybe God did, and you don't know."

"You know, I prayed for a Division I scholarship and didn't get one."

"But you met me."

"I know... but I stopped praying."

"I know."

"I mean Pete didn't pray for his mom to beat cancer, right?" Choker says.

"Yeah, he told me he figured there were enough people praying and if that wasn't good enough, then God didn't want his mom to live."

"Yeah, and that is why I didn't pray to God for Pete to be found in the ocean" Choker says. "I

THE CHESS GAME

mean, how many good people does God need praying for someone to answer the prayers?

"Is it like a game, a basketball game? Do you need a hundred people? A thousand? A million?

"Why do some parents leave the Ronald McDonald House with healthy cured kids while other parents leave without their kids? Did those parents not pray hard enough? Did the parents holding their bouncy kid's hand pray harder?"

"No Rochambeau," Cresty says. "Remember, God doesn't play games."

"Not even chess?"

"Not even the Game of Chess," she says.

A man with an orange jiff hat and a bottle in a bag in one hand is pushing a walker with the other on the red stone path next to the asphalt drive. He stops in front of the sign: DR. ULYSSES SIMPSON WIGGINS.

He points to a state police boat in the harbor, actually two of them, saying, "Thankfully, the law is here."

He opens the bottle and offers us a swig as the marine cops board the red-white tanker anchored in the river. Cresty offers him some M&Ms.

"In the early 1800's, horse teams walked around this oval to propel the ferry across the river," he says. "They had to stop the service for lunch to feed the horses."

"Makes sense," Choker says.

"Hah. No one could cross the river when the mules ate," Cresty says. "The people couldn't paddle their own rafts down river... they needed mules."

"Horses. The ferry boats all had names," the orange jiff hat man continues. "Names like the Phoenix and the Constitution. One was called Moses. And another the Independence, I think."

"Makes sense," Cresty says. "To name them, I mean."

We sit below some trees on the hill facing the Wiggins Park sign and watch the man in the jiff hat share the bottle with our sailor guide right in front of the window washer who just stares into the grimy glass. We can see Philly's City Hall where Ben Franklin preached Colonial unity with William Penn on top pointing out behind the Moshulu, but we can't see beyond the Ben Franklin Bridge.

Cliff sends the chess moves: Qc4 Qh5

We walk on a new stone crosswalk. We stop to buy water from a street vendor with beads around his neck and his cart's FRESH FRUIT SALAD sign crossed out.

On his radio plays U2's 40:

THE CHESS GAME

> I waited patiently for the Lord.
> He inclined and heard my cry.
> He brought me up out of the pit
> Out of the *Camden* clay.
>
> *Will the king,* sing a new song.
> *Will the king,* sing a new song.
> How long to sing this song?

Cresty injects, "How long will we wait for the Lord?"
Choker strums the guitar and sings:

> How long to sing this song?
> How long, how long, how long
> How long to sing this song?
>
> You set my feet upon *Camden*
> And made my footsteps firm
> Many will see, many will see and hear.

Choker strums harder on the guitar. Twirling the beads around his neck, the vendor sings with him:

> *Will the king,* sing a new song
> *Will the king,* sing a new song

Will the king, sing a new song
Will the king, sing a new song
They all sing. I wish I could sing with them.

How long *will the king* sing this song?
How long *will the king* sing this song?
How long *will the king* sing this song?
How long *will the king* sing this song?

The vendor hands us three bottles of water, although Choker only asked for two.

"Forty," he says, "as in Psalm 40."

The vendor pushes his cart to the orange building and shares the bottle with the man in the jiff hat and our sailor guide. But the window washer with a camouflage yellow jacket and reading glasses just stares into the grimy glass facing the river.

THE CHESS GAME

Chapter 17

We will be returning home. Together. With the three-string guitar in tow.

The parking attendant and the doctor drive our truck down to the river from Cooper Hospital.

Choker and Cresty thank them. They tell us that dropping the truck off here was no problem since the boat Doc lives on is docked in the Wiggins Marina.

In front of the orange building, the doctor hands some pills to the vendor, who extends three water bottles out to them. There is one for the man in the jiff hat and one for our sailor guide but the window washer doesn't reach out for his. Wali, the parking attendant, declines an offer from us to drive him back to the garage.

So, we drive south on Broadway.

"See that," Cresty yells, pointing down Mechanic Street toward the river.

"I'm driving," Choker tells her. "I'm looking ahead so I don't run down anyone."

"Stop. Backup. Go down Mechanic Street,' Cresty orders. "I think I saw the black stovepipe hat."

Choker Obeys. He slowly drives down Mechanic. He stops at 308. There is a booth in front of the house. The booth is guarded by a man in an official looking red beret. Yo-Yo is sitting in the booth with the metal red roof in front of the boarded-up home.

"What you say you doing here," Yo-Yo stammers, leaving the booth and walking toward us.

"Truthfully," Choker begins to say.

"Yeah, truthfully," Yo-Yo snaps back.

"Truthfully," Choker says, "I was planning to ask you that."

"You drove here to ask me that?" Yo-Yo questions.

"No, Yo-Yo," Cresty says in a reassuring tone. "I thought I saw a black stovepipe hat, well the top of the hat, head this way when we past the street."

"Oh, no worries," Yo-Yo says. "You know it is Bloom's Day back in Ireland? Must be one of the kids playing dress up…"

"Sounds better than one of Booth's Avengers patrolling the street," Choker smirks. "So what's up with you here?"

"I guard the house where Boston Corbett lived," Yo-Yo says while adjusting his red beret. "He also lived on 328 Pine Street, but no one knows that, not even the Booth Avengers, so we don't guard it anymore... anyway it is a Methodist Church now... so God guards the grounds."

We make a right on Broadway and drive past the trash-to-steam plant that is built only blocks away from the Maritime Museum, where a group of young teenagers with paint-spotted Urban Promise t-shirts are building three wooden sailboats. They work under a statue of a man holding a pole with an American flag above his head and a dog looking admiringly up at him. The names of the three boats, 15-footers and double square ended with a bare sail mast in the middle, are freshly painted on the sterns: Faith. Hope. Promise.

Behind the teens, nailed to the wooden red double door, is a fundraising poster for an upcoming event of Msgr. Doyle seated in a rowboat named "Do Your Bit." The smiling priest is paddling under the Ben Franklin Bridge, pulling mightily on both oars.

We stop at the statue of Matthew Henson and his dog. Cresty googles his name. She shows Choker the phone screen. He reads, "An African-American Explorer."

Swiftly, Cresty tells us how Henson was on Admiral Robert Peary's famed 1909 expedition to the North Pole... how Peary tired... how Henson carried him… how Henson actually passed the geographically point of the North Pole and when he doubled back to get Peary, he saw his footprints… how realizing he was the first man on the North Pole stuck the pole with the American flag in the ice… how he went back to get Peary resting on the dog sled… how Peary was credited in history for reaching the pole first…

We slow down passing Sacred Heart Church, lowering our dirty windows, hoping to see Monsignor Doyle, but we are overwhelmed by the stench coming from the ugly orange trash burning facility.

We drive past blocks and blocks of open fields, boarded up row houses, and homes with satellite dishes on the small porch roofs.

We drive faster past Morgan Village, which connects into Fairview Village from a bridge. A church is situated, well, rises on the bank of the small stream. It is called the Bridge of Peace Church.

A man at the bottom of the bridge has his hand out. It is the postman who looks like he isn't many years from retirement. He isn't still carrying his sagging flat mailbag on his shoulder, but he is wearing his polished shiny shoes from earlier this morning.

THE CHESS GAME

"Hey there again," He says, "Yorkship Village was the first federally funded planned community for residents of the working class in the United States. It is now called Fairview. The village was designed by a guy named Darwin. He was influenced by the "garden city" developments of France."

"I don't have any money to give you for the info," Choker says, slapping his outstretched hand. "But, if you play chess, use the French Defense."

"Not money for info," the postman says, "but for surviving Camden."

"Give him your jersey," Cresty says. "Number seven didn't bring us any luck finding the chess piece."

Choker peels off the jersey and gives it to the postman.

"Did you know seven is a biblical number?" Cresty asks. "It means perfection ... like Camden again someday."

"I know numbers, but I didn't know that," the postman says. "Ask me any zip code. Ask me any seven zip codes in the country."

"El Paso?" Choker asks.

"79835," he answers.

"Tucson?" Cresty asks.

"85701," he answers.

"The Bronx?" Cresty asks again.

"10451," he answers. "Home of the Yankees."

"Bend, Oregon?" Choker asks.

"97701," he answers.

"South Bend?" Cresty asks.

"46601," he answers. "Home of the Fighting Irish."

"Cambridge?" Choker asks.

"02138," he answers.

"Camden?" Cresty asks.

"29020."

We drive half a block to Ironside Street in Fairview, which is flanked with boarded up homes. That's when Cliff sends the chess moves: h3 Bxh3.

Ruby says into the speakerphone, "I'd hope, by giving you Ruby's pair of red sneakers, you'd find the king."

"But, you gave your pair of red sneakers to the man with the Abe Lincoln black stovepipe top hat," Cresty protests slightly.

"No," Ruby says, "I gave *you* Ruby's pair of red sneakers… when you give to one in need you give to all… no?"

"No worries," says Choker. "We won't be seeing the Wizard here in Fairview."

"Never, ever stop'd looking, ever, never," Ruby says. "Hey, hope ya'll see all the streets, how'd the streets have names, named after famous ships.

THE CHESS GAME

About a thousand homes were built after World War I near the old New York Shipbuilding Company of Camden."

"We're looking for *the streets with no names*," Choker says. "Where Bono is."

"None of the streets, though, are named after the USS Indy," Cliff says. "I do want to add, though, about the location of the wreck. She was never found, as if the Indy didn't sink, like it never happened. But listen to the ghosts of Fairview, they will tell you they built the USS Indy… and they will tell you what the Indy did… and they might just tell you the Indy was cursed for carrying the bomb… and how Camden is cursed for building the boat that carried death."

"Hey, tell me, what is the zip code of Camden?" Choker asks.

"08101," Cliff says. "Why?"

"No reason, but the postman said it was 29020. Listen, I learned to play your guitar," Choker says. He strums and sings U2's Iris:

> The star
> That gives us light
> Has been gone a while
> But it's not an illusion
> The *break*

In my heart
Is so much a part of who I am
Something in *our* eyes
Took a thousand years to get here

The postman at the bottom of the bridge yells, "It seems like it has taken Camden a thousand years to get here."

Choker backs up the truck and says, "Or a thousand beers... hey, tell me, you said Camden's zip code was 29020."

"It is," he says. "Camden, South Carolina."

"What is Camden's zip?"

"04843."

"No, its not," Choker says. "Its 08101."

"Oh, Camden, New Jersey," the postman says. "I thought you meant Camden, Maine... 04843."

"Yah, Camden, New Jersey is 08101," the postman says smiling.

"Tell me then," Choker says. "Do you feel Camden is cursed?"

"Camden?" the postman asks. "Camden, South Carolina?"

"No, Camden."

"Camden, Maine?" he asks.

"Yup. Camden, Maine," Choker agrees.

"No. I don't think Camden, Maine is cursed or

THE CHESS GAME

Camden, South Carolina," the postman says.
Choker strums and sings:

> Something in your eyes
> Took a thousand years, a thousand years
> Hold me close, hold me close and don't let me go
> Hold me close like I'm someone that you might know
> Hold me close the darkness just lets us see
> Who we are
> I've got your *strife* inside of me
> *Eyes... eyes...*

The postman walks back to his post at the bottom of the bridge and says, "I got your lucky number seven jersey to bring luck to Camden... New Jersey." Choker gives him the double thumbs up and sings:

> Once we are born, we begin to *regret*
> The very *treason of shame*
> But you
> I'm sure I've met
> Long before the night the stars went out
> *Guilt* meeting up again
> Hold me close, hold me close and don't let

me go
Hold me close like I'm someone that you might know
Hold me close *as* darkness just lets us see

Cresty, smiling and sleepy, closes in, holding us all. Choker strums harder and sings louder with the music coming from his phone:

Who we are
I've got your life inside of me
Iris... Iris...
The stars are bright but do they know
The universe is beautiful but *old*
You took me by the hand
I thought that I was leading you
But it was you made me your man
Machine
I *scream*
Where you are
Iris standing in the hall
She tells me I can do it all
Iris wakes to my nightmares
Don't fear the world it isn't there
Iris playing on the *stand*
She buries the boy beneath the sand
Iris says that I will be the death of her

THE CHESS GAME

> It was not me
> Iris… Iris…
> Free yourself, to *see* yourself if only you could *be* yourself
> Free yourself, to be yourself if only you could see…

"You know," Cresty says, squeezing us harder. "Iris is Bono's mother and the song is about how he can still feel her love for him… like the light that reaches Camden from a burned out star."

"Do you mean Camden, New Jersey?" Choker asks smiling.

We're all smiling now. Maybe I should call Cresty Iris. I want to be Bono.

"But the song stops, the words stop about being so feel good," Cresty continues. "Bono wanders. He goes from comforting by his mom in the sky to confusion, to sadness. His own spiritual journey is endless and ceaseless with rambling thoughts about questioning his own faith… the journey exhausts him, too."

The postman hustles behind them.

"I don't think Camden is cursed either," he says. "You know General Horatio Gates lost the Battle of Camden to the Brits and Cornwalls…"

"Cornwallis," Choker and Cresty say together.

"You know," the postman continues, "if he, Horatio, didn't blow the Battle of Camden and won, he would've been the first president of the United States... not Washington."

"So how is that good for Camden?" Choker asks.

"Well its good for Camden, New Jersey because the Battle of Camden was in South Carolina... see if it was here, well Camden would've been cursed with life's 'what if,' the biggest curse of them all..."

"What do you mean?" Cresty asks.

"Well," the postman started, "Eulace Peacock's family moved from Alabama to Union, New Jersey when he was a kid. He played football for Pop Warner at Temple in Philly and he ran track.

"Peacock beat Jesse Owens in 1935 on July 4 in Lincoln, Nebraska."

"So?" Choker says. "Did they wear the Lincoln stovepipe hats when they ran?"

"No, it's the great 'what if,'" the postman continued. "In the spring of 1936, Eulace tore his hamstring at the Penn Relays in Philly, he crossed the bridge here in Camden, back to his home in New Jersey and couldn't run in the 1936 Summer Olympics in Berlin where Jesse Owens won four

THE CHESS GAME

gold medals and debunked Hitler's propaganda of Aryan Supremacy.

"Owens became known as the "World's Greatest Athlete" ... Hitler, he was named Time Magazine's 'Man of the Year' in 193... there were no Olympics in 1940 and 1944 because of the war... Peacock faded into history's 'what ifs' with his journey across the bridge back into Camden..."

"Are you saying, what if the people of Camden did something... did something differently... did something now?" Cresty asks.

Speeding away in his postal truck, the postman pumps the breaks and stops at the bottom of the bridge. He comes over and asks, "Tell me, what are you really doing here?"

Choker spins toward him, leans out the window and says, "Listen, I was in Ireland for my 18th birthday and to go there on the cheap I signed up with some of her Dad's boys for an old-folks tour, figuring I didn't have to go with the group and stop every place.

"I was in Donegal and on the ride to Derry the van stopped at Belleek. The old people got out to see the crystal factory. I asked the tour leader if I could take the van up north in the mountains. He told me to be back in an hour and a half.

"I drove for 45 minutes and turned around. But

right before the turnaround it started getting windy and snow flurries were landing. I saw this guy carrying a big black bag... like your postal bag but larger and not as flat.

"On the way back, I asked him if he wanted a ride. He jumped in and thanked me, putting the big black bag between the seats. We started talking and soon enough we were like old brothers. His name was Paddy."

"Well, *meself* and Paddy hit it off. He invited me to his daughter's wedding that summer. I told him he would be there. Then I asked him, 'what was in the big black bag?' He looked at me with disfavor and said 'none of your business.'

"I drove a few miles and then said, 'Paddy, sorry about asking about the big black bag, but...' and he interrupted and stared at me in the eyes and said, 'none of your business.'

"A few blocks before we get to the crystal factory, at a stop sign, I turned to Paddy and said, 'really, I'm sorry...' then he turned away from me and screamed, 'none of your business' and hopped out of the van.

"I was pretty shaken as I pulled into the factory parking lot. I was glad when the old people started coming out. When the tour driver came to the door, I hopped over the seat... kicking the big, black

THE CHESS GAME

bag… Paddy left his big, black bag."

Choker leans back in the window, the postman grabs Choker's shoulder and asks, "So what was in the big, black bag?"

Choker spins around and leans back out the window. He looks the postman in the eyes with a death stare.

"The king," Choker says, driving away and down another street of Fairview Village named after a sunken ship.

Crossing over South Constitution Road, the street Cliff lives on, Choker mumbles to himself, "I gave him my number seven jersey but we never found the king."

"Yeah," Cresty says, "But you have a three-string guitar … that you know how to play already."

THE CHESS GAME

Chapter 18

The twilight sun reflects off the rusting wrought iron 4-foot spiked fence that surrounds the cemetery.

"You know why there is a fence around this graveyard?" Choker asks.

"Na."

"People are dying to get in," Choker laughs flipping up the mirror sunglasses and playfully tapping me. "That one never gets old. Does it?"

"Na."

We turn at what we think is the main entrance. A gray brick arch, like a tower, leads to a narrow asphalt road.

A sign reads there are maps at the office of HISTORIC HARLEIGH CEMETERy. We won't need a sign to find the famous Walt Whitman's grave, I think.

Cresty reads her phone: "It says the cemetery is designed as a park, like a Victoria-era garden cemetery, for a place of public entertainment... for the people."

At the front gate, patrolling... rather gliding... Mornie... the guy who was under the clock selling used photos of former Hollywood stars. He is riding his motorized mini-scooter with the cannon pointing away from the gate. Carrying the portable CD playing samba music with the whistle replacing the piano keystrokes of the song "Clocks," he stares ahead, as frozen as the clock stuck on 10:10.

"Shhhh with the cussin," Mornie hushes, turning and pointing the cannon on the front of the seat of the motorized mini-scooter at us, and then says, "Evenin."

We pay no attention to Mornie. We are here to find Walt.

We make a left on a hilly narrow path toward a lower lake in the middle of the cemetery. There is a small island in the middle of the lake with three trees spaced evenly apart. At the bottom of the hill, in front of a mausoleum that reads DAVID BAIRD, a boy with blonde bangs shooting straight under an olive-green army helmet, the canvas straps hanging from both sides, swipes the hair from his eyes and gently spins around.

Three white-jumpsuit dressed workers in a white double-cab pickup truck slow down, only to stare at us. We can see the back of the truck is loaded up with birdseed. Beyond the truck, a smaller lake nestles next to the big lake. Behind the smaller lake there is a lone stone outhouse, which is in front of a hilly mound covered with leaves and a dozen trees.

In front of us, a man with a ragged beard

wearing a spiffy blue suit thoughtlessly lifts up his right arm and flicks a tree branch, knocking off a leaf. He turns backwards, fumbling his satchel a bit, and mouths the word, "sorry" to us but with no sound.

There are mausoleums dug into a mound to our right, the one facing the large lake. We turn right and cross a road that divides the lake and continue driving in the back of the cemetery that is bordered by the winding, murky Cooper River.

The paved road is choppy and narrow and marked with potholes and bordered by old, leaning trees. We turn back to the left and see a meter maid dressed in a tight-fitting blue uniform. She is holding the hand of a young girl. Her preschool daughter?

At a roundabout, we turn around between the river and the first one of the lakes. From a patch of mud, a flock of geese squawk at us on the highroad overlooking the river. The geese stop their squawking as a college-looking girl and a guy, who looks younger than she is and is carrying a stack of books, walk by holding hands. They are dressed in colorful and light clothing. The gaggle of geese fly away. Mud flaps from their wings as they fly over the girl and guy. Somehow none lands on their colorful clothing, or on their shoes, and they walk away like they will be happy the rest of their lives.

Cresty is reading her phone, while standing next to a black metal trashcan. She tells us how this back section is the "Veteran's plots section of the cemetery," which peacefully is overlooking the river. From across the potholed street, a man walks toward us with a blank face and plucks a plastic white bag that is tied at the top out of the trashcan next to us. The man walks back across the bumpy street. On the back of his black hoodie reads the white letters: Hank's Restaurant.

Checking us out, the three white-jumpsuit dressed workers in a white double-cab pickup truck whip down the potholed street. They barely miss running over a girl dressed in all black with white headphones dangling from her ears who doesn't slow down and doesn't break her stride. She is chatting into her phone... but no... she is making no sounds.

Looking to our left, Cresty points over to the Vietnam cemetery, which is dotted with black marble tombstones and is jammed in the center between the Vets plots and that lone stone outhouse near the backside mound... where now the hitchhiker with the Yankees hat on sideways stands in a pile of leaves that surround his sneakers without laces. The circular and yellowish leaves

THE CHESS GAME

look like used condoms.

Beyond the lone stone hut rises Our Lady of Lourdes Hospital... and the Blessed Mother overlooking the mound and the lake... and the Vets and Vietnamers. Small birds suddenly twirl and fly right toward us and over a lady dressed nicely in all black using an umbrella as a cane. The lady doesn't flinch.

We backtrack to where the offices are located and to the main gate that looks like a fortress opening without the drawbridge. A pregnant woman in a short black skirt and high heels walks in through the entrance holding an empty lemon Gatorade bottle.

"Lost?" Cresty asks, but the lady just walks by us.

We drive around the small oval, or roundabout, where a family of four with the mother wearing a shroud stands in front of the quiet office.

We drive down a path overlooking the smallest of the three lakes where there are four early-teenage girls line dancing behind the small lake. The youngest girl is out of step but she can't hide her frozen smile.

We make a left down the hill facing the little lake and then bear left where there is a flowering yellow tree at the foot of the path. But three orange cones block the road. A lady, sitting on the stump of the middle mausoleum and holding a baby, looks up. She looks exactly like Cresty. Red hair tied in ponytail. Even her shoulders are strong like her jaw. We can't drive beyond the cones.

We back up the path, past three identical looking mausoleums that we didn't notice and drive back up the hill as a man in a yellow jacket, with the slogan KEEPING CAMDEN CLEAN AND SAFE on the bottom of the back in black letters, walks down the hill. He isn't pushing a yellow trashcan on wheels and doesn't have the name Caesar stitched on the front of his jacket.

We park at the main office that is still quiet and still empty except for the one guy in gray suit that is sitting on the stoop with no shoes. Just socks.

We can see a stone house of a grave tucked into the recess of the hill with only smaller stone blocks around it facing a hill.

We walk down the hill facing the concrete building tucked neatly into the earth. There is a grass field that is open in front of it and at the bottom of the hill we see a stone staircase that we had missed.

On top of the mound, a young dark-haired and mustached man with a slight smile, like Mona Lisa, is looking down admiringly. A noisy backhoe

THE CHESS GAME

backs up into the equipment garage behind him.

On top of the stone house is the Abe Lincoln black stovepipe top hat.

The grave's roof is pointed and below the ridge is a name engraved simply in stone: WALT WHITMAN.

There is a also a black stone etched with his likeness. It shows a full flowing white beard, like the one we saw in his photo with Peter Doyle in the hallway of his house.

The inscription reads: WALT WHITMAN MAY 31, 1819 - MARCH 26, 1892

Below his timeline reads:

> AUTHOR OF LEAVES OF GRASS THE MOST EXTRAORDINARY PIECE OF WIT AND WISDOM THAT AMERICA HAS YET CONTRIBUTED. HIS LIFE WAS IN A FERMENTATION OF FREEDOM. HIS POETRY WAS THE CELEBRATION OF LIFE AND FREEDOM AND WAS A PREPARATION FOR DEATH …

We can't read the rest of the epitaph. The words are faded above the etching of the man with his white beard.

White stones lay on either side of two trees that

flank his tomb, leading us to the entrance. There is another tree to the right that is carved with initials of worshippers, or perhaps just visitors drinking on the shady hill, as high as you can reach.

Thick stones of black blocks surround the mausoleum.

Inside of a black gate at the opening... he is buried among his relatives.

Walt.

We found Walt.

There are no other graves in the area. The stone blocks we saw on the hill across from us are just stones. Above his tomb is another tree carved with initials.

We can see the statue of the Blessed Mary above us.

The leaves that cover the mound are layered.

Choker edges toward the gate of black iron that protects the entrance; a small American flag hangs on the gate.

Inside the gate is... the king.

The chess piece king is in front of Walt Whitman's grave inside the stone building.

The three white-outfitted workers in the white double-cab pickup truck stop behind us.

All at once, the three workers say, "Congrats. You found the king... no one comes here anymore.

THE CHESS GAME

Congratulations."

Etched in small letters on the base of the king are the words: "Resurgemus - we will rise again; the martyrs will live."

Cresty says, "Ruby wanted us to have it."

With trembling hands, Cresty looks up Resurgemus on her phone. Her voice cracks as she reads Walt Whitman's poem:

> *Suddenly, out of its state and drowsy air, the air of slaves,*
> *Like lightning Europe le'pt forth,*
> *Sombre, superb and terrible,*
> *As Ahimoth, brother of Death.*
> *God, 'twas delicious!*
> *That brief, tight, glorious grip*
> *Upon the throats of kings.*
> *You liars paid to defile the People ...*
>
> *The bullets of tyrants are flying,*
> *The creatures of power laugh aloud:*
> *And all these things bear fruits, and they are good.*
> *Those corpses of young men,*
> *Those martyrs that hang from the gibbets,*
> *Those hearts pierced by the grey lead,*
> *Cold and motionless as they seem,*

Live elsewhere with undying vitality;
They live in other young men, O, kings,

We walk back toward the lower lake in the middle of the cemetery with the small island. We stop at the bottom of the hill, in front of the mausoleum that reads DAVID BAIRD. The boy with blonde bangs shooting straight under an olive-green army helmet is gone.

"Baird Boulevard," Choker says, "where the strip joints were razed…"

"Where no businesses have risen," Cresty adds.

Kissing the king, Choker holds the chess piece above the water. The reflection doesn't shine through the king. The holes in the pumice piece are filled with dirt, packed with grit.

"The king can float to the island, live between the trees," Choker says. "Return to an island… an island like where the pumice was found by Cliff's father while stationed in the Mariana Islands."

"Like an arch-ipe-lago," Cresty stutters, "that rose from volcanoes on the ocean floor."

Choker places the king on the water edge.

The king sinks.

"But pumice is hardened lava," Choker protests, "pumice floats."

"But pumice lives unattached," Cresty injects,

THE CHESS GAME

"Attached to a rock, pumice sinks... like it does when packed with dirt"

Mornie wheels up behind us. He lifts his right leg over the seat of his motorized ride. He slides off the mini-scooter. He crawls, pulling himself with his arms to the lake's edge. He reaches into the lake with a splash. He pokes his right hand, taking a few stabs into the water. He pulls out the king. He shakes the water off the king.

"The king is a miracle... the king floats," Mornie says, turning back to us, "Really, the king was floating... just like the stars on Hollywood Boulevard... you're a miracle if you survive the streets of Camden... if you survive, you're a miracle... I swear to you."

Mornie rubs the king with water from the lake cupped in his right hand. He rubs but the dirt doesn't budge from the holes. He places the king on his scooter. He slides over and unties Choker's thick-soled hiking boots. He slides off Cresty's ruby-red sneakers. He pulls off their socks. Cupping his hands, he washes their tired feet.

Choker reaches for the king. He sits on the mini-scooter and laces up his thick-soled hiking boots. We walk up the narrow path, back toward Walt. Cresty carries Ruby's sneakers. At the top of the hill, we turn back and see Mornie floating on his back in the lower lake. He paddles with his cupped hands toward the island. At the land's edge, he pulls himself up and crawls in front of the three trees spaced evenly apart. He spreads out.

Kissing the chess piece, Choker places the king back inside the tomb, saying, "So he, the king, is then all those people we met on the street of Camden today, according to Walt."

"Right," Cresty says. "The Camdeners."

"The Wizard, then, is Everyman, too, the people of Camden need to rise up," Choker says. "The Methadonians need to rise with the Camdeners."

"Right," Cresty says. "Walt knew… he wrote the truth over 100-some years ago, without even the internet… he used his imagination to write the truth… man, Fr. Doyle knew, too."

Reading from the phone, Cresty and Choker recite the rest of Resurgemus:

> *They live in brothers, again ready to defy you;*
> *They were purified by death,*
> *They were taught and exalted.*
> *Not a grave of those slaughtered ones,*
> *But is growing its seed of freedom,*
> *In its turn to bear seed,*
> *Which the winds shall carry afar and resow,*

THE CHESS GAME

And the rain nourish.
Not a disembodied spirit
Can the weapon of tyrants let loose,
But it shall stalk invisibly over the earth,
Whispering, counseling, cautioning.
Liberty, let others despair of thee,
But I will never despair of thee:
Is the house shut? Is the master away?
Nevertheless, be ready, be not weary of watching,
He will surely return; his messengers come anon.

The three white-outfitted workers in the white double-cab pickup truck pull closer behind us... edging closer.

"Huh? What's you talking about?" The driver asks. "Walt wrote an elegy, O Captain, My Captain, to the assassination of Lincoln. That's his masterpiece. Not the chess piece."

"Right, not the chess piece, but Resurgemus," Cresty corrects him.

The worker in the passenger seat says: "Yeah, no, Walt's masterpiece is called When Lilacs Last in the Dooryard Bloom."

The worker in the back seat says: "Don't get too deep... when Walt wrote about Lincoln, citing the

Lilacs, Venus and Hermit Thrush, he was equating nature to the Trinity."

The driver says: "Lilacs are wild, usually past the human habitat, gray brownish, leaves are bright green and arranged in opposite…

The worker in the passenger seat interrupts: "Venus is the second planet from the sun, rotates in opposite direction of most other planets, earth's "sister planet…"

The worker in the back seat says: "The Hermit thrush is a bird with a white eye ring and a song that is the finest in nature, flute like beginning than several descending notes, related by harmonic simple integer pitch rates like most human music… my wife feeds them downtown… the Hermit thrush is the symbol of America's voice…"

"No, you don't understand," Choker insists. "You. You three are the king. You and the people of Camden… all of the Camdeners."

"Huh?" they say together.

"We're not that smart, but we know when we hear one, a lovely tribute to Lincoln," the driver says. "You know, his friend, Walt's friend Peter Doyle was an eyewitness to the Lincoln assassination."

"Our baby will be no Lincoln," Choker says.

"How," Cresty says, "do you know?"

THE CHESS GAME

"Maybe," Choker says, "he will grow up to be as good of a man, though, as Father Doyle, Mannion and McDermott... The Three Monsignors."

We drive along the rusting wrought iron 4-foot spiked fence that surrounds the cemetery.

"You know why there is a fence around this graveyard?" Choker asks again.

"Na."

"People are dying to get in," Choker laughs, playfully tapping me again... until he sees a DOT worker in an orange hoodie with a large orange juice container... who cut us off... and continues.

We turn at what we think is the main entrance. A gray brick arch, like a tower, leads to a narrow asphalt road. But the gate is locked.

A sign reads there are maps at the office of HISTORIC HARLEIGH CEMETERy. We follow the arrow on the sign.

We drive past the main office that is still quiet and still empty except for one man in a gray suit who is sitting on the stoop with no shoes, just socks ... and a window washer with a camouflage yellow jacket and reading glasses standing in front of a grimy window facing Walt.

Choker stops driving and walks over to the man in the gray suit. He reaches out to put the mirror sunglasses on the man's face and rests them on the bridge of his nose. But the glasses fall off. The mirror lenses shatter on the stoop.

Driving out of South Camden, down 676, we see a sign for the Walt Whitman Bridge. The last of the setting sun, nearing the longest day of the year, reflects off the clouds behind the glowing green Philly skyscrapers. There is a hole in one cloud through which light pours down on the far tower of the Walt Whitman Bridge.

Choker calls Ruby: "Good one Rube - t*he King bridges people*. The Walt Whitman Bridge… I get it… but Walt Whitman says the people are the king … not the king."

"And, the good Monsignor Doyle would add," Cresty says, "like the jurors in the Camden 28 trial were the kings."

"The people have to be the kings," Ruby says. "Good Monsignor Doyle is battling jaw cancer… and good Monsignor Mannion was transferred from the Cathedral… and good Monsignor McDermott is battling … battling to remember.

"The Three Monsignors will be gone someday from Camden, too, just like The Three Mayors… but for different reasons… but for the people they will all be gone."

THE CHESS GAME

    On the ride down the Atlantic City Expressway, Choker sings U2's I Still Haven't Found What I'm Looking For:

> I have climbed *city hall tower*
> I have run through *shields*
> Only to be with you
> Only to be with you
> I have run, I have crawled
> I have *feared our* city *hall*
> Said it was
> Only to be with you

    "Ya. Bono, with all his fame and money, is looking for Jesus. Just like us," Cresty says. "Just like the people."
    "But we found the king," Choker laughs.
    They both sing:

> But *we* still haven't found what *we're* looking for
> But *we* still haven't found what *we're* looking for

    Choker stops singing. He asks, "Could this… this day… this all … " before Cresty says, "You mean this… this all be Rochambeau? Just luck?"

KEVIN CALLAHAN

He sings:

> I have kissed *money's* lips
> Felt the healing in *His* fingertips
> It burned like fire
> This burning desire
> I have spoken with the tongue of angels
> I have held *the imprinted shroud*
> It was warm in the night
> I *so* cold as a *bar*

They look at each other and both ask, "Luck?" They both say "Johnny Luckett …"
They sing:

> But *we* still haven't found what *we're* looking for
> But *we* still haven't found what *we're* looking for

Cresty strums on the three-string guitar and continues to sing. I sing along:

> I believe in *Camden* come
> When all the *people* were bleeding as one
> Bleeding *as* one
> Yes, I'm still running
> He broke the bounds, he loose the *thorns*

THE CHESS GAME

> Carried the cross of my shame
> Shed my shame
> You know I believed it
> But *we* still haven't found what *we're* looking for
> But *we* still haven't found what *we're* looking for
> But *we* still haven't found what *we're* looking for
> But *we* still haven't found what *we're* looking for

We all lie down on the low bunk on the boat in Cape May. They won't want to bring me into this world, I think.

I always wanted to be more than just the boy who isn't alive yet in the black and white, fuzzy photograph taken of me today... to be alive.

I want the chance to, to be a king, too. To be the people. But I don't know. Do they know?

Cliff texts: Qd5 Bf5# CHECKMATE

We wonder if Ruby moved out of turn. He always wins... right?

Choker turns on his phone and sings U2's Beautiful Day:

> It's *another* day

Sky falls, you feel like
It's *another* day
You just can't get away

I do know that the view from the hospital window showed me a new world in an old city on this beautiful day.

I am the tight-roper. I can still picture the scene down the street, even in the darkness, two men sitting at a table.

Looking across, I see the 'R' building... and the yellowish-brown brick building with slotted windows... I don't have to look up at the City Hall clock... I look down to the spire of the Cathedral below the clock where the rising moon reflects off the gold cross and onto the steps below.

A crumpled-up pamphlet is blowing and bouncing around the steps. The curled-up man with the eye patch unfolds the ball and reads: "The question is whether you choose to disturb the world around you, or if you choose to let it go on as if you had never arrived." – Ann Patchett

The eye patch man whispers to himself, "Johnny Luckett ... mother ... Patchett."

I guess, like Bono sings, "If you want to kiss the sky, you better learn how to kneel."

THE CHESS GAME

From my tight rope view, I look back down Benson Street.

Under a hanging light bulb on the porch, Cliff moves a piece on a board, saying "*blooming* day to be alive."

With his sneaker-less feet, Ruby swipes all the other pieces off the black and white checkered board… except the missing king.

END

www.ingramcontent.com/pod-product-compliance
Lightning Source LLC
Chambersburg PA
CBHW020350170426
43200CB00005B/114